<u>Breeding Your Budgerigars</u>

A Guide of How to Start Up Your Own Breeding Aviary

With Tips on Aviary Construction, Cages, Birds to Pick, Possible Setbacks, hatching and Any Ailments Your Birds May Pick Up

British Library Cataloguing-in-Publication Data
A catalogue record for this book is available from
the British Library

Contents

HOUSING THE BUDGERIGAR

ALMOST too well-known for description to be necessary, the Budgerigar, up to the period of the last war when feeding difficulties became acute, was almost as ubiquitous as the Canary.

Seen caged in countless households where its playful habits, its art of mimicry and its capacity for imitating the human voice made it one of the most engaging of pets, it is bred on a modest scale by many hundreds of enthusiasts and to a greater extent by many others.

As a garden ornament, an aviary filled with many coloured Budgerigars is indeed a striking picture and youngsters indulging in their playful antics are a ceaseless source of entertainment.

A member of the Grass Parakeet family and a native of the grass lands of Australia, the Budgerigar in the wild state feeds on seeding grasses of all kinds and nests in hollows in the Eucalyptus tree where, during the breeding season, they congregate in large numbers.

About 7½in. long, the wild type Budgerigar is of a bright green colour on the breast, head and face yellow with black throat spots and wings with wavy black markings on a yellow ground and a longish dark green tail; many other brilliant colours have been developed from the normal Light Green.

Possessing the usual powerful Parrot-like beak and sturdy legs with four claws, two pointing forward and two backwards, eminently suitable for climbing, the sexes can be distinguished by the wattle or cere, the fleshy, somewhat heart-shaped adornment situated immediately above the beak. In the cock Budgerigar this is blue, whilst in the hen it is whitish to nut brown, but the shades vary according to the condition of the bird; in sickness the cere of both cock and hen pales considerably and in some instances the cere of the hen changes to a pale blue, recovering its normal shade on the return of the bird to a fit condition.

Amenable either to cage or to outdoor aviary, the Budgerigar needs no artificial heat to keep it in condition and its food requirements are simple in the extreme, whilst normally it is a singularly trouble-free bird and, kept under hygienic management, enjoys life to the full, bursting with energy and vitality. It is particularly suitable for the man with limited means and garden space as the cost of upkeep is quite small and elaborate birdrooms are not essential.

Sometimes referred to as a Lovebird, a misnomer, the Budgerigar has no connection with this species, being of an entirely different family and habitat.

The all-important question of providing the very best accommodation for one's stock is inevitably bound up with the amount of garden space available and the amount one is prepared to lay out on a birdroom and flights. Of course, if a spare room in the house is available as a breeding room and this is light and airy, one only needs to erect outside flights and shelter but whatever type of structure is decided upon, there are certain golden rules which must be observed.

Firstly, Budgerigars, whilst able to withstand any amount of static cold, do not like cold winds, draughts or damp, in fact all these conditions are deleterious to their well-being; therefore, flights should face south or west with, in an exposed situation, protection at the sides from cutting winds.

Secondly, shelter must be provided in order that the birds can obtain shade on hot, sunny days, although they appreciate the beneficial effects of the milder sun during spring and autumn.

Thirdly, all structures should be made vermin proof as rats and mice can do an immense amount of harm once they obtain access and it is easier to build them out than it is to keep them out once they find their way in. Cats, too, must be guarded against as they also can inflict damage and badly scare the inmates of an aviary.

Bearing these important points in mind, attention must next be given to the type of base on which the birdroom and flights will stand. Cement is undoubtedly the best for all purposes but is probably the most expensive. In view of the advantages of such a floor, the outlay is probably worth while. Paving stones make an admirable base, as also do well laid bricks and all such floors are easy to clean and are vermin proof.

If cement is used, provision must be made for disposing of rainwater and this can be done by laying the floor on a slight slope at the bottom of which a channel can be made to carry away the water after heavy showers. The framework of the flight will of course bridge the channel which should not be large enough to permit the entrance of mice. A paving or brick floor requires no provision for carrying away rainwater as this will soak away between the interstices and if well laid on sand or on fine ashes will give no subsequent trouble.

Structural materials can next be considered and here let me say that unwise economy at this stage may lead to rueful expenditure later; therefore make sure that whatever material is used is satisfactory for the job it has to do.

Flight construction presents no difficulties, the easiest method being to first make a series of wooden frames of the required dimensions from 1½in. × 1½in. timber, cover them with ½in. mesh wire netting

Breeding room constructed with asbestos sheets. The windows are placed at the top, thus conserving wall space for breeding pens

Outside flights of neat design arranged in L-shaped formation

This extremely neat birdroom and flight is ideal for the small garden

In contrasting style a range of double-decker breeding compartments

and bolt or screw them together to form the flight, the top of which can be made on a frame of lighter material, e.g. 1½in. × 1in.

It should be borne in mind that wire netting is sold in regular widths, 1ft., 2ft., 3ft., etc., and the strengthening spars of the aviary frames should be so spaced to avoid wastage of wire netting which should be of good quality and free from blobs of galvanising material. Budgerigars will attempt to pick these off with disastrous results.

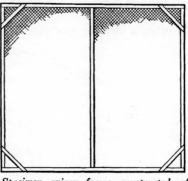

As ½in. netting is not mouse-proof, it is an advantage to board up the bottom 3ft. of the flights with matchboarding or, if obtainable, sheet iron can be used and painted on the outside and the cost so incurred will be saved on wire netting, but if food is never placed in the flights but always provided in the bird-room, there is little danger from mice. However, it should be

Specimen aviary frame constructed of 1½in. × 1½in. batten. The corner battens are recessed ¾in.

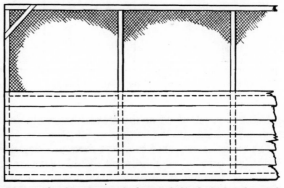

stressed here that food con-taminated with mouse drop-pings or wet-tings can have serious and sometimes fatal effects, there-fore everything possible should be done to keep these pests out.

All outside woodwork should be well

Section of aviary frame, the bottom half of which is boarded or covered with iron or asbestos sheets

creosoted and left to dry for a day or so before the birds come into contact with it, and one most important point to remember in con-nection with wire netting is never under any circumstances allow jagged ends to be exposed. Cover them with narrow battens such as trellis laths and so avoid the possibility of a bird being caught by its leg ring with the certain prospect of serious injury or death. It is better to fix the netting on the outside of the aviary frames although there are certain circumstances where netting on the inside is unavoidable.

A final word in connection with flights. Give as long a flight as possible, 9ft. minimum if room is available; width and height are not so important.

Dealing with the birdroom itself, line drawings are appended of two types of combined breeding room and flights. Both are recommended and whilst one is suitable for a somewhat sheltered situation, the other is ideal for an exposed position. Details of a simple flight

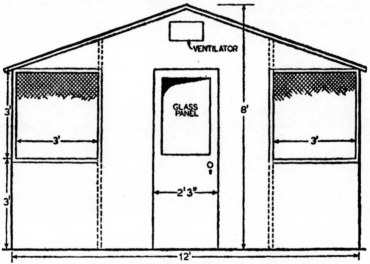

Fig. A (1): Front section of the combined breeding room and flights for an exposed situation. The window spaces are covered with ½in. wire netting

and shelter required when the breeder possesses an indoor breeding room are also shown.

The reader is not asked to accept these as a dogmatic idea of how a Budgerigar breeding establishment should be constructed but they are set out as thoroughly recommended designs, combining cheapness, compactness and ease of management with efficiency and leave nothing to be desired. Should the potential breeder adopt either of them, it will be found that there is no great difficulty in their construction, but if so desired a shed of the requisite size can be purchased from one of the mass producers of these articles and the necessary alterations carried out. Here I should point out that the sizes shown are purely provisional but are the minimum recommended for overall efficiency.

Framework should be of 2in. × 2in. timber and if the structure is made in sections and bolted together, will give corner posts of 4in. × 2in.

Regarding material for covering the sides and ends, ordinary weather board is *not* suitable as it is not draughtproof and does not give a flush interior surface which is necessary in connection with the fitting of the interior breeding pens, etc. Tongued and grooved matchboarding ⅜in. thick is quite suitable, but the best type of covering is ship-lap, a type of moulded and rebated weather board which combines a pleasing exterior appearance with a perfectly flush fitting and flat interior surface, the cost being approximately the same as matchboarding.

Ordinary floor boards, about ½in. thick, can be used for the roof,

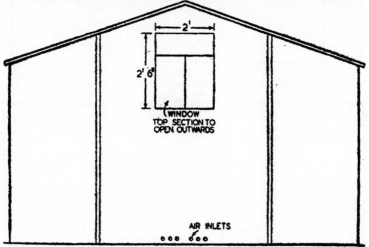

Fig. A (2): The rear section of the combined breeding room and flights for an exposed position. The window may with advantage be made considerably larger

which should be covered with a good quality roofing felt, and a wooden floor can be added although if the birdroom stands on a cement or similar base this is not essential.

The main requirements of a birdroom are adequate space and airiness combined with freedom from draughts and damp with plenty of light, but at the same time the minimum amount of glass should be used in order to maintain an equable temperature and finally, adequate ventilation is most essential.

All glass should be covered on the inside with ½in. netting on removable frames in order that windows may be opened without the fear of any bird which may have found temporary freedom in the birdroom escaping, and as a prevention against such a bird dashing itself against the glass in its efforts to escape and possibly sustaining injury.

The accompanying line drawings are more or less self-explanatory but a few notes on them will no doubt be of assistance.

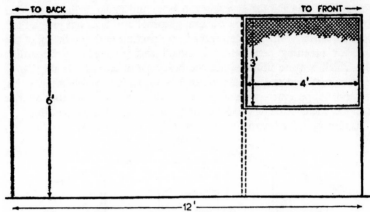

Fig. A (3): *Side section of the enclosure for an exposed situation*

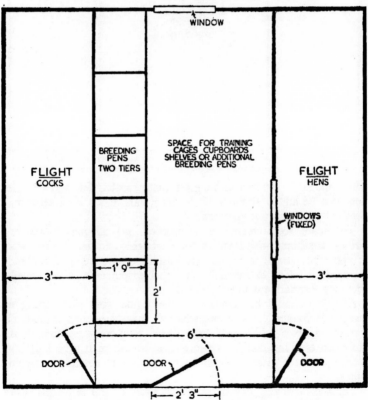

Fig. A (4): *Plan of the suggested layout of the combined birdroom and aviary*

Fig. A (1-4) depicts a span roofed combined breeding room and flights suitable for an exposed situation, overall dimensions 12ft. × 12ft. and furnishes an interior room 12ft. × 6ft. with a flight 12ft. × 3ft. along each side, almost wholly covered in. These should be lime-washed inside. The layout is very compact but allows ample length of flight, provision for 10 or more breeding pens and room for training cages, cupboards, shelves, table and additional breeding pens if required.

The front section as shown in Fig. A (1) requires little comment except that the glass panel in the door is recommended to furnish extra light in the breeding room and also to enable one to observe if any bird should be loose before the door is opened. The ventilator above the door should be placed as high as possible and can be made by simply cutting a rectangular hole in the woodwork and covering with perforated zinc both inside and outside and finishing off at the edges with a strip of neat beading.

Fig. A (2) shows the rear end of the structure and needs little explanation, being a solid end broken only by the window and the air inlet at the bottom which can take the form of six or seven 2in. diameter holes drilled through the woodwork and again covered inside and out with perforated zinc. The sides as shown in Fig. A (3) need no comment, although a window might be fitted in each of the sides, towards the back ends, to provide more light inside the flights.

The plan as in Fig. A (4) shows the suggested layout with doors to each flight from inside the breeding room. These doors can be made with the top portion of wire netting which will give more air in the breeding room and will provide observation into the flights. The partitions, reaching the whole length of the structure and erected from floor to roof on the breeding room side of the necessary framing, can be constructed of thin matchboarding, plywood, Essex board or other similar material and on to one of these partitions the breeding pens can be built, these being described in another chapter.

The opposite partition can be utilised for a number of purposes as shown in the diagram and contains a fixed window to furnish additional light. Show cages, etc., can be stored in their cases underneath the breeding pens and there is ample room for seed bins, etc.

The interior of the breeding room can be finished with a flat leadless oil paint, limewash, creosote or white Aviary paint, a special preparation harmless to birds, at the breeder's pleasure and for protection at night and during inclement weather, frames fitted with glass or Windolite can be constructed to fit over the outside of the flight wire netting. These can easily be kept in place by turnbuttons fixed to a fillet of wood of the same thickness as the frames, screwed above and below the wire netting at the same distance apart as the size of the frame. They are most useful in boisterous weather.

The second series of line drawings Figs. B (1–4) depict another type of birdroom and flights more suitable for a sheltered situation. The breeding room is of the lean-to type with outside uncovered flights and is less expensive to construct than the span roof structure. Overall measurements are 14ft. × 12ft.

Fig. B (1) shows the appearance of the front of the breeding room before the outside flights are fitted. The ventilator can be made in the same way as in the previous type of birdroom described and details of the bob-holes and landing flaps are shown in Fig. C. When open, the landing flaps are kept in a horizontal position by an iron bracket screwed underneath and by arranging a flap both inside and outside of the birdroom wall the birds can either be shut in or out. This is a great convenience when cleaning out and when catching up birds.

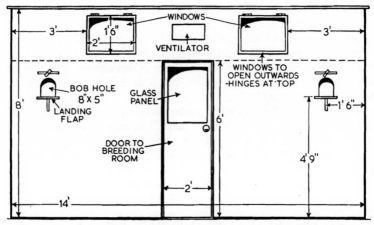

Fig. B (1): Front of the combined breeding room and aviary designed for a sheltered position before the flights are fitted

Fig. B (2) shows the outside flights fitted to the front of the breeding room and the lengths of the flights can be varied according to the amount of space available. They can be constructed of aviary frames and are shown as completely open although the bottom half may be boarded in as previously shown in the diagram of aviary frames.

A frame door opens into a passageway to the breeding room door, bounded on each side by the wire netting of each flight and the top of this passageway should be covered with ½in. wire netting in the same manner as the tops of the flights. This outer door should be fitted with a spring so that it automatically closes.

The sides are shown in Fig. B (3) and need no comment except that the air inlets should be provided on both sides. The back of the breeding room is a solid section 14ft. × 7ft. The plan of the whole

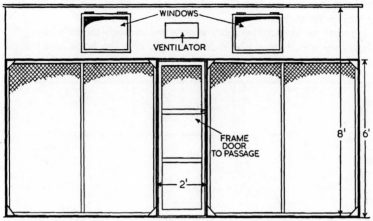

Fig. B (2): *The front of the breeding room after the flights have been attached*

structure is shown in Fig. B (4) and provides an interior breeding room 8ft. × 6ft. with space for eight breeding pens, cupboards, etc. Two inside flights are also provided, each 6ft. × 3ft. with a frame door opening into each from the breeding room. These flights are simply made by erecting a partition of ½in. netting covered aviary frames from

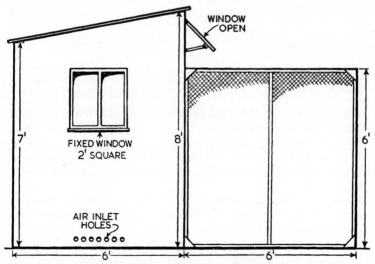

Fig. B (3): *Side elevation of the structure. The length of the flights attached can be varied according to the space available*

floor to roof the whole width of the breeding room. A fixed window is shown on each side.

Access to the outside flights is obtained through the bob-holes, the flaps over which should be closed at night after the birds have settled down in the inside flights.

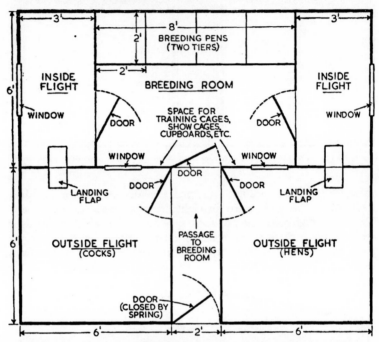

Fig. B (4): Plan of the combined breeding room and aviary for a sheltered position. The room accommodates eight breeding pens and two inside flights. The size of all windows is the minimum recommended. They can be larger

A frame door opens from the passageway into each outside flight.

Fig. D is a representation (not to scale) of an inexpensive structure comprising flights and shelters only with no provision for breeding. This type of aviary is all that is necessary if an indoor breeding room is utilised and it will be seen that the flights are separated by a wire netting frame.

The shelters also are partitioned off by means of matchboarding or plywood so that cocks and hens are housed separately. Dimensions of the shelter are 7ft. high in front, 6ft. at back, 6ft. wide and 4ft. 6in. deep. Each shelter has a door to open outwards into the flight and this is fitted with a bob-hole and landing flap. Doors can be kept open during the day in hot weather and ventilation is provided for in both shelters as shown in the diagram. The doors, bob-holes and windows should be closed at night of course.

The separate flights fitted to the front of the shelters are shown as completely open with a safety door opening outwards at the end of one flight, across which, 2ft. in, is the door to the flight proper, with a door to the other flight on the left. Doors are again of ½in. netting on frames and if so desired the safety arrangement can be built outside the end of one flight so that no length in the flight is lost. This, however, does not present such a neat layout and more material is required.

The structures described in this chapter may seem rather costly to erect but, bearing in mind that they have been designed giving foremost consideration to efficiency with ease of management, the initial cost will be thoroughly justified and as they leave nothing to be desired subsequent alterations with their additional expenditure will be unnecessary. If all outside woodwork is creosoted and interiors renovated yearly, repairs will be reduced to a minimum.

The wire netting may be preserved if desired by painting both sides with black enamel (*not paint*). This not only enhances the appearance of the aviary but also enables the birds to be seen more clearly as the dazzle from the netting is obliterated.

It will be observed that all tiresome stooping in order to enter flights has been obviated in these designs and the layout in each case so arranged that the chances of a bird escaping are negligible. It should, however, be pointed out that if under any circumstances the entrance to a flight is constructed without a safety door, the entrance door should be low, about 3ft. 6in., and should open outwards.

It will also be noticed that in all three designs provision is made for cocks and hens to be housed separately. This is very desirable as will be shown in a later chapter.

Finally, as a protection against cats, should they abound in

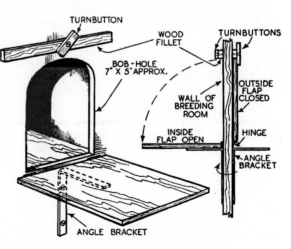

Fig. C: Bob-hole and landing flap

one's neighbourhood, double netting can be used on aviary frames and this should consist of ½in. mesh on the inside and 1in. mesh on the outside. To prevent cats walking on the top of open topped flights strips of thin plywood studded with tin-tacks can be nailed along the top edges of the aviary framing with the business ends of the tin-tacks uppermost.

It will be found that cats object to walking on wire netting and once they find they are unable to negotiate the tops of the aviary frames

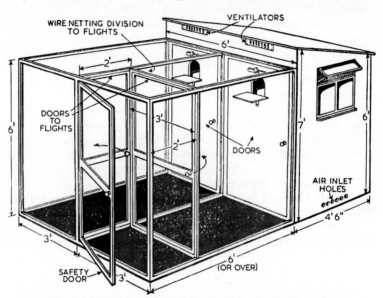

Fig. D: Inexpensive aviary with no provision for breeding pairs

they will soon leave the inmates unmolested. Should the birdroom be situated close to a road or public path, it is advisable to cover any windows on the outside with wire netting in order to avoid breakages by stones which may be thrown by mischievous lads.

Suitable substitutes for wood in the construction of birdrooms are flat asbestos sheeting, hardboard and similar material and a very satisfactory building can be erected on a wooden framework using these substances for covering. Flat asbestos sheets on the outside, the interior being lined with hardboard, completes a birdroom which is superior in some respects to one constructed with matchboarding.

APPLIANCES

Perches, Seed, Water and Grit Vessels, Seed hopper, Greenstuff holders, Nest boxes

THE appliances and gadgets used in Budgerigar keeping and breeding are many and varied and descriptions of the most necessary and most commonly used must next receive consideration. There is unlimited scope for improvisation in this direction and the breeder with an inventive turn of mind will find much with which to exercise his or her ingenuity.

Perches. These should be of $\frac{1}{2}$in. round softwood and the material sold as curtain or dowelling rod is quite suitable provided it is not painted, but in flights it is an advantage to instal natural perches in order to provide change of grip and consequent rest for the birds' feet. Apple boughs or hazel branches commonly used for peasticks are eminently suitable, but laurel, privet or yew must be avoided.

Seed, water and grit pots. Any kind of shallow, easily cleaned receptacle can be used for these purposes but they should be of glass or glazed earthenware for preference and a tour of Woolworths will provide a wide choice of such articles. Preserve pots, used for various foodstuffs, will be found useful but avoid deep dishes of any kind as not only does the seed at the bottom of these remain untouched but if used for water there is a danger of young Budgerigars becoming totally immersed and possibly drowned.

Seed hopper. An aid to easy management is provided by the use of seed hoppers which are obtainable in various sizes from any pet store, or one can quite easily be made from a wooden box as shown in the illustration. A hopper of the dimensions shown will hold about 7lb. of seed and will require no attention once it is filled until the husk drawer requires emptying or the hopper needs re-filling.

The glass front should be fixed at an angle by means of small wooden strips with a stop at the bottom and it should reach from the top front of the box, resting on a cross strip, and should extend to within $\frac{1}{2}$in. of the back of the box about 9in. down from the top. A feeding trough, 1in. deep and 1in. wide, must be fixed underneath the seed outlet and care must be taken to see that the top edge of the feeding trough is level with or slightly higher than the bottom of the glass, otherwise the seed will overflow into the husk drawer and will be wasted.

The trough can be made either of wood or of zinc and if the former material is used it is an asset to make the bottom of very fine mesh such as is used in a flour sifter. This will keep the trough free from dust which will drop through into the husk drawer. A perch should be fixed across the box, level with and about 1½in. in front of the feeding trough.

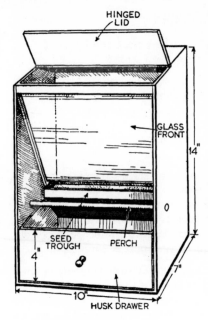

Greenstuff holders. For the accommodation of greenstuff in an aviary, hanging wire baskets should be provided and those commonly used for ferns or for small creeping plants are ideal for the purpose. Wire netting can, however, be shaped to fulfil a similar purpose, but all ends of the wire should be carefully trimmed off so that there is no danger of a bird being caught up by its leg ring.

Greenstuff holders for use in breeding cages or pens can also be made in a similar manner and so shaped that they can be fixed to and hang flat against the netting or cage front.

Home-made seed hopper

Cuttle-fish bone can be pierced and hung up with a short length of thick wire or can be wedged behind a 6in. length of curtain taut stretched across the cage front and fastened with the usual hooks.

Various cleaning utensils will recommend themselves to the breeder and among these an ordinary paint scraper and a soft paint brush will be found extremely handy for cleaning out cages and pens. An old teaspoon forms a very satisfactory tool for cleaning concave bottoms of nest boxes described later in this chapter and a cobbler's or lino knife with a hooked blade is admirable for scraping perches.

Nest boxes. Budgerigars are not particular as to what type of nest box is provided for their domestic activities but a correct size entrance hole and loose concave bottom on which to deposit their eggs are necessities. No nesting material is required.

There are a number of types of nest box available but the old-fashioned cocoanut husk is most definitely not recommended owing to the inconvenience one is put to in inspecting the interior and also to the difficulty incurred in keeping it clean. Some of the types advertised are quite elaborate in construction whilst others are perfectly simple to make from ⅜in. or ½in. wood but it is not proposed to describe them all, details of two only well tried and thoroughly recommended patterns being provided (see diagrams).

Fig. E shows a box within a box, the interior portion being open topped and sliding into the outer receptacle, its normal position being pushed right in. The interior box has the entrance hole at the front and is fitted with stepping block and loose concave bottom. When it is desired to inspect the interior, a finger is inserted into the entrance hole and the inner box carefully withdrawn. The hen, if within, will fly out into the

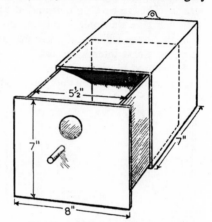

Fig. E: Draw-out type of nest box

cage or pen and the eggs can be inspected or the youngsters examined.

Fig. F depicts an entirely different type of nest box, equally efficient, and very little description is necessary apart from that given in the diagram. The small perch at the entrance hole should be of ½in. diameter and about 2in. long and should not project beyond the inner side of the nest box otherwise the youngsters will scramble out prematurely. Budgerigars like a fairly close fitting entrance hole and this should be from 1¼in. to 1½in. in diameter. The loose concave bottoms, supplied in various sizes but generally 5in. square, should be at least 1in. thick.

When constructing nest boxes care should be taken to see that the stepping block and concave bottom fit fairly close to each other and to the ends and sides of the box, gaps being a danger to the young chicks, but they should not fit too tightly or difficulty may be

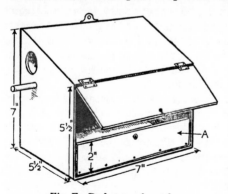

Fig. F: Desk type of nest box

experienced in removing them for cleaning, due to possible swelling through moisture when in use. The best plan to adopt when fitting one-self out with a supply of nest boxes, if it is intended to make them, is to purchase a number of loose concave bottoms all of the same size and then to make a similar number of stepping blocks of the same width as the concave bottoms but about ½in. thicker and approximately 2in. deep. The concave bottom and stepping block when placed side by side will give the interior dimensions of the bottom of the nest box and all boxes will be of identical measurements and concaves and stepping blocks interchangeable.

A stepping block is simply a piece of softwood cut as described in the preceding paragraph and placed on the floor of the nest box under-

neath the entrance hole. With this in use, there is less danger of eggs being broken, as the hen will scramble through the entrance hole on to the stepping block and can then walk carefully on to the eggs resting on the concave bottom.

The stepping block is cut from thicker wood than the concave in order to prevent eggs from being scattered out of the latter and so becoming cold. The stepping block also provides material for the

Interior of nest box. Note position of concave bottom and stepping block in relation to entrance hole

hen's gnawing propensities, much in evidence when about to lay.

The loose concave bottom should be smoothly finished and not too shallow, but at the same time the depth of wood at the thinnest part of the bottom should be not less than ½in. As a general rule, the type of nest box as depicted in Fig. E is most suitable for use in breeding pens or flights where there is room to put down the interior when taken out for inspection and that as shown in Fig. F, possessing a large hinged flap, allows of easy access to the eggs or youngsters when used inside breeding cages which do not lend themselves to the bodily removal of the nest box or its interior.

The draw-out type of nest box can also be constructed lengthwise, i.e., one side containing the entrance hole and perch and forming the front of the box. Such a box does not project so far out into the breeding quarters and is equally as efficient as the type illustrated.

In these types of nest box the interior should slide *loosely* into the outer box, as during the breeding period the box sometimes swells with moisture and will stick.

BREEDING

BUDGERIGARS are most obliging creatures in anything connected with the propagation of their species and will, provided they are in fit condition, breed at any time during the year and will continue to lay clutch after clutch as long as the nest box is left in position and the pair are kept together. Obviously, a tremendous strain would be thrown on the birds if such a state of affairs was allowed to continue and would probably terminate with the death of the birds through exhaustion, therefore a wise practice, and that generally followed, is to allow the parents to rear two rounds of youngsters only each year and to limit the number of chicks per nest to four.

It is as well to note that it is the rearing of chicks that throws such a strain on the birds, not the process of egg laying and incubating. If, therefore, the first round results in only one or two chicks being hatched and reared and the second produces only a similar number, a third round may be taken, but no pair should be allowed to rear more than eight or nine young in any one year.

When to commence. The normal breeding season for Budgerigars kept in captivity is early spring, although some breeders commence operations early in the New Year in order that the youngsters may be fully moulted out into their adult plumage by the time the Young Stock Shows promoted by all Cage Bird Societies are held in June, July, and August and also in order that, if desired, the youngsters can be used for breeding in the following year.

Although early breeding has its advantages, it is not recommended to the beginner who should adhere to the stereotyped principles until experience has been gained. There is little doubt that early hatched youngsters are generally superior to those that are hatched late in the year, but whether they are better than those bred round about the normal hatching period, i.e., April or May, is a debatable point.

Birds paired up in December and January to produce youngsters from then onwards must in themselves be vigorous and sturdy to be able to carry out their domestic affairs during the worst months of the year with their cold spells, drying easterly winds and cold, wet periods together with absence of sunshine and short daylight hours and it therefore follows that youngsters hatched and surviving under such conditions must in their turn also be strong and healthy.

Budgerigars do feed their chicks after daylight has gone but it must be realised that once the cock has fed the hen for the night and filled up its own crop, that supply of food has to last the family until daylight and the cock is able to see to partake of a fresh supply from the seed pot, and when it is remembered that in December and January there are approximately 14 hours of darkness each night, it can be understood that early breeding is something in the nature of an experiment.

The use of artificial light certainly enables the hours of darkness to be reduced and the youngsters to be fed at a later hour but this does not overcome all the drawbacks to very early breeding which, when conducted under adverse weather conditions, does sometimes bring its trials and tribulations in the nature of chills, egg-binding, etc., which the beginner is ill-equipped to meet and disappointment is likely to be felt when losses are experienced among the very young chicks.

Whilst early hatched youngsters generally commence their moult into adult plumage at an early stage and are fully moulted by the time the Young Stock Shows come along and do go a long way towards completing their development before the trying hot summer weather arrives, too early breeding often produces a disappointing first round, therefore the beginner is advised to wait until the more favourable weather arrives, and the middle of March is quite early enough for the birds to commence their domestic activities.

At the same time it must be realised that no hard and fast rule can be laid down as to when breeding should commence. This obviously depends on whether the birds are in breeding condition or not, and if a certain pair with which it is desired to breed show obvious signs of desiring to go to nest very early in the year, it would be unwise to hold them back and, conversely, it is equally foolish to pair up birds at any time in the year if they are not in breeding condition. The obvious procedure then is to wait until the birds are ready to breed and this can be ascertained merely by observation.

Breeding condition. Presuming the cocks and hens to be housed separately, the symptoms of breeding condition are just a little more difficult for the uninitiated to perceive than is the case when all the birds are kept together, a procedure with which I am not in favour.

The cocks will be seen to be bursting with vim and vigour with cere a bright blue. They will beat a tattoo on the perches with their beaks, at the same time uttering their somewhat warbling love song, and they will also regurgitate food from their crops and feed the wire netting with it. Obviously fighting fit, they will indulge in minor squabbles (cocks never quarrel seriously), and often two of them will

Metal and fountain type seed hoppers

Some essential utensils in the Budgie breeding room

The correct way to hold a Budgerigar to prevent it biting

Left: The type of breeding pen preferred by the Author. Below: Budgerigar breeding quarters of alternative design

chatter away to each other at the same time tapping their beaks together quite violently. Sometimes they will feed each other. If the cocks and hens are separated only by wire netting the cocks will continually fly from perches to netting and feed the hens through the holes, the hens meanwhile clinging to the netting awaiting their attentions.

The condition of the hen is more important, it being most unwise to allow her to go to nest until she is ready. If put in the breeding pen too soon, failure to lay or egg-binding may result. When ready to breed, the hens will exhibit a rich, deep brown cere and they will gnaw the woodwork of the flights and will sometimes lay eggs in odd and unexpected corners such as the husk drawer of a seed hopper. If they are able to see the cocks, they will be continually clinging to the wire netting, calling to them and will, by their generally restless behaviour, exhibit their desire to go to nest. The condition of the cere is in itself a fairly good guide, a hen with a whitish or a pale-coloured cere rarely being ready to breed. The same applies to the cocks, a bright blue cere being evidence of high condition.

If the cocks and hens are housed together the symptoms of breeding condition will be quite obvious. The birds will pair up and will constantly fly together, the cock will feed the hen and mating will take place.

Additional feeding. When the breeder is fairly certain that the birds are approaching breeding condition, cod liver oil prepared seed as described in Chapter 3 may be given for about a fortnight prior to the birds being placed in the breeding pens. If this has already been fed to the birds during the winter months and has not been discontinued, this is all to the good, but it is as well to place it before the birds every day at this period. Certain precautions should be taken when using cod liver oil. The best plan is to prepare the seed every other day or so, and the cod liver oil bottle should be kept out of the light, in a cupboard for instance. The proportions as laid down in Chapter 3 should not be exceeded.

Fresh chickweed daily is a help towards fertility and should certainly be sought and fed to the birds when they are coming into breeding condition, although this does not mean that it should not be given at any other time. An occasional millet spray also helps towards conditioning the birds.

The breeder's aim should be to bring his breeding stock to the highest possible state of fitness in readiness for the subsequent somewhat arduous time ahead when families are being reared. Cuttlefish bone and/or old mortar should have been available to the birds during the whole year. Failure to provide this will probably result in soft-shelled eggs.

Pairing. It cannot be too strongly emphasised that the selection of an appropriate partner for any bird is of the utmost importance, and only too often is it found that insufficient care has been taken in this direction, resulting in disappointing youngsters. Breeders must realise that the type of offspring that will be produced is decided immediately a pair is placed in the breeding pen, therefore do not be too hasty in pairing up and study the pedigree as well as the visible features of any bird with which it is desired to breed. If the bird has been used in a previous season, those records should also be consulted to see if any undesirable traits were encountered during its former breeding activities.

I would point out at this stage that a single pair of Budgerigars will seldom breed. Being gregarious by nature they prefer to conduct their domestic affairs in company and two or more pairs will go to nest readily providing they are in sight or sound of each other.

Budgerigar cocks should not be used for breeding until they are at least eleven months old, whilst hens should be a little older and should certainly not be mated under a twelvemonth, neither should hens be used if they are too fat, otherwise egg-binding may result.

Hens appear to be at their best in their second year, but thereafter they do not always perform their maternal duties in a satisfactory manner, sometimes being rather negligent towards their offspring. I would advise against using a hen for breeding after she has passed her third year unless she possesses outstanding properties. When breeding from old hens I would certainly use foster parents, the advantages of which will be discussed later in the chapter.

I have known Budgerigar cocks perform their paternal duties in a satisfactory manner at the age of eight years, but I consider them to be at their most vigorous from a twelvemonth up to the age of four years. It is a good plan when arranging pairs to endeavour to mate a young bird to another which has had previous breeding experience, and so obtain a pairing in which inexperience but youthful vigour on the one hand is counterbalanced by maturity and knowledge on the other.

Never attempt to pair up birds which are moulting or which are in bad or weakly condition or which have ailed in their younger days. To do so is only inviting further trouble with the possibility of losing a bird, therefore see that all breeding pairs are in perfect health and do not use any birds possessing deformities such as overgrown beak or rickety legs.

Neither should birds with any organic disorder or growth be used for breeding, but missing toes or claws or any other disfigurements caused by accident are not transmittable to the offspring and birds so damaged may safely be used for breeding provided they are otherwise in good health. Budgerigars which have lost a leg have been known to produce youngsters and to rear them quite satisfactorily.

The aim of every breeder should be to produce youngsters better than their parents and so raise the general quality of the stock. By judicious selection of breeding pairs, the elimination of all specimens not up to standard and by the continuance of the blood of an outstanding bird throughout the best of its progeny, this can be successfully accomplished *provided the initial stock is of good quality*. Breeders who commence and continue on these lines will seldom need to make fresh purchases.

As a general rule, the breeder will not go far wrong if he chooses good big hens with large heads and no major faults and pairs them to well-made, shapely cocks or, to put it briefly, size in the hen with type in the cock. But guard against using any birds which are small and lack substance. Of course, the breeder will desire to produce youngsters of a certain colour and this aspect will be dealt with in a later chapter on the recognised colour varieties, but the general rules relating to pairing are applicable in all cases.

The desirable features which the breeder should seek to reproduce and improve are type, substance, large round head with largish round throat spots, rich colour, correct wing carriage and markings and an alert, upright posture. To this end I would advise against the use of any birds which lack substance; those with small, mean looking heads, also birds with tiny throat spots, or with the two centre spots perceptibly smaller than the others, this being a difficult fault to eradicate. Bad colouring and bad wing carriage can be corrected to a certain extent by selecting a partner with characteristics the reverse of those in the birds possessing the fault or faults.

Further undesirable features are protruding beak, a hollow or break in the outline at the back of the neck, known to breeders as " nipped in the neck ", and a humpy carriage, giving the bird the appearance of being round shouldered. All these failings are difficult to breed out and it is far better not to use such birds for breeding.

The beginner may well ask what is meant by " type " in a Budgerigar and this is by no means an easy question to answer. The breeder with a " fancier's eye " spots a " typey " bird in any collection imme-diately he sets eyes on the birds, and such a specimen is typical of the species, possessing no major faults but exhibiting all the desirable characteristics embodied in the Budgerigar Society's standard for the ideal Budgerigar.

In effect, a bird possessing type is intensely pleasing to the eye, with no obvious faults but with its good qualities so perfectly blended that none predominate, the whole make-up presenting a perfectly balanced specimen of a Budgerigar. Such birds are priceless to the breeder who should never falter in his quest to produce their like.

Pair good birds to others of similar quality, therefore, and do not waste an outstanding cock on a mediocre hen or vice versa. Such pairings will only produce moderate youngsters, something of an average of the quality of the two parents, and such a procedure will, if persisted in, eventually lower the standard of the whole stock.

Pick out the best bird of the desired colour, then, be it either cock or hen, select the best suitably coloured specimen of the opposite sex and place them each in a show cage or in any other suitable box cage and compare the two closely. Pay particular attention to size and shape, the size and shape of head, mask and spots, colour and wing markings and carriage, and place a value on these characteristics in the same order of preference as they are set out here.

If both birds happen to possess the same minor fault, e.g., a slight falling away at the back of the skull, badly shaped throat spots or crossed wing tips, bear in mind that these faults will be intensified in the progeny and do not use the birds under inspection as a pair. Other partners must be found for them, but should the two birds both exhibit the necessary desirable qualities and are both free from major faults without both possessing the same minor blemishes, they may safely be paired with the probability of producing good quality youngsters.

Carry on with this procedure with the second best bird and so on until the desired number of pairs has been selected or until it is found that the remaining birds are not of sufficiently high quality to be considered for breeding.

From the remaining birds, however, it is wise to select one or two pairs for use as foster parents, their quality or lack of it being immaterial provided they are healthy. It is an advantage to know if these particular birds are good parents, one of the reasons why detailed breeding records should be kept, as will be discussed later. These birds for use as foster parents can be paired up at the same time as the other birds and they will be used to rear chicks from overcrowded nests or from exhibition parents which the breeder does not wish to subject to the strain of raising a family.

It may be well to summarise the main points which must be adhered to in order to pair up birds with the probability of desirable youngsters being produced and, in addition, a few useful hints are also tabulated.

1. Never use birds for breeding which are not in breeding condition.
2. Do not use birds which are too.young.
3. Avoid using stock which is or has been ailing, is moulting or out of condition.
4. Do not use a hen which is too fat.
5. Birds possessing deformities or growths or which are suffering from disease should on no account be bred with.

6. Endeavour to select large hens and shapely cocks possessing substance.

7. Never pair birds both exhibiting the same fault or both lacking the same desirable characteristic.

8. Avoid using birds with small heads.

9. Do not pair birds both of which possess very large throat spots or multi-spotted youngsters will result. Pair such large spotted birds to others with good, but not over-large spots.

10. Avoid using birds with tiny or with badly shaped throat spots.

11. A bird with crossed wing tips should be mated to one with slightly drooping wings, whilst a bird with short wings should be mated to another with longish wings.

12. Always aim at producing rich, even-coloured youngsters and avoid patchiness and lack of depth.

If the cocks and hens have been housed together, it will be necessary either to separate them for at least a fortnight before breeding commences or to catch up the potential pairs and cage each pair for a similar period. This must be done in order to prevent fertilisation taking place by a cock other than the one chosen for a particular hen.

The birds being in breeding condition and the pairs arranged either mentally or on paper, the next step can be proceeded with, and this consists of the actual mating which should be conducted as now described.

Mating. Breeding pens or cages should be prepared for the reception of the pairs by being thoroughly cleaned and provided with nest box, seed, fresh water, grit, cuttle-fish bone or old mortar and greenfood. The nest boxes should previously have been scoured with *boiling* soda water and left to dry out, this treatment effectively dealing with red mite or any other pests which may have been present in the crevices of the woodwork.

See that the loose concave bottom in the nest box is fairly smooth and spread a *little* fine pine sawdust or fine peat moss litter all over the bottom. This will fill any gaps between the concave and the sides and ends of the nest box, and so prevent tiny youngsters coming to grief therein, and will also absorb any droppings, although most hens keep their boxes fairly clean.

The nest box should be fixed as high as conveniently possible, bearing in mind that it must be easily accessible for examination and cleaning out, and avoid placing it so that the entrance hole faces a dark corner. Do not fix a perch too close to the entrance hole, 6in. is quite near enough, otherwise first round youngsters will clamber in and out of the nest box much to the annoyance of the hen whilst she is laying her second clutch of eggs and trouble will probably arise.

A perch too close to the entrance hole of the nest box is also an inducement to youngsters to leave the box prematurely.

See that all perches are fixed securely, otherwise incomplete mating will occur with resultant clear eggs. Place seed pots, etc., as far away from the nest box as possible, so that the maximum amount of exercise is obtained by the birds but, at the same time, do not place any vessels underneath perches where they would become fouled.

All being ready for the introduction of the pairs, the hens should first be caught up and placed in their respective pens and allowed five minutes or so to settle down. Watch them during this interval, and should they show curiosity towards the nest box, this is a good sign. If in advanced breeding condition they will examine the box all round and will peer in through the entrance hole, taking the greatest interest in what will be their future abode. Do not be discouraged, however, if the hen should sit quietly on the perch without showing the slightest sign of interest in the nest box. She may merely be awaiting the presence of the cock to stimulate her into acute curiosity.

Next catch up the cocks and quietly place them each with his future spouse. Stand still, away from the birds, and watch quietly. If the breeder's judgment has been sound and the birds are in breeding condition, love-making will commence almost immediately, the cock chattering to and perhaps feeding the hen and endeavouring to entice her into the nest box. The actual mating should take place within a very few minutes, but should this not occur and the pair appear to be friendly, all will probably be well and the pair may be safely left together.

Should they fail to take the slightest notice of each other, however, it is best to replace them in the aviary for a day or so, as this is a sign that either one or both of the birds is not yet ready to breed, and I do not believe in trying to force matters.

A hen may sometimes display animosity towards a cock when he is first introduced to her, and in this case it is as well to leave them together for a day or so to see if matters improve. The hen may be in breeding condition, but, not favouring that particular cock, will keep him at a distance for a time, though eventually allowing him to conduct his love-making.

After mating has taken place, the hen will constantly clamber in and out of the nest box, generally gnawing such woodwork therein as is accessible and, gradually spending more time in the box each day, will prepare for the important business of raising a family. At this time, the cock will be seen feeding her through the entrance hole of the nest box, and this he does by regurgitating food from his crop and passing it on to the hen by placing his beak in a scissors-like manner across the mandibles of the hen and then, by a pumping-like action of the neck, forcing the food into her beak.

Soon the hen will become swollen around the vent, exhibiting prominence behind the legs and her droppings will become more fluid and very copious. This is a sure sign that the first egg is on the way and it may be expected about the eighth day after mating has taken place.

It is a sound policy not to mate up all the pairs at the same time, but to allow a few days to elapse after putting up two or three pairs and then follow on with another few pairs and so on. By this means, should a sudden cold, dry spell occur with its possibilities of causing egg-binding or dead-in-shell or colds, etc., all the pairs will not be similarly affected, as they will be in varying stages of their domestic activities and the possibility of inclement weather seriously endangering the results from all the pairs is avoided. Birds for use as foster parents should be mated at the same time as the first breeding pairs.

Where cocks and hens have been kept together during the year and have been paired up in cages for a week or so prior to the commencement of breeding, if the actual breeding cages or pens have been used for this purpose it is only necessary to place the nest box in position after the requisite length of time has elapsed, and the pairs will normally carry on with their business of raising a family. I would, however, state that it has been my experience that matters proceed much more rapidly when the sexes have been kept apart throughout the year.

Recording. It is necessary at this stage to commence keeping records of the breeding pairs, as all serious breeders do, and I think no better system can be devised than that of breeding cards combined with a stock register. A breeding card can be affixed to each pen or kept elsewhere in the birdroom and can be ruled out on a postcard in the following manner :

Pair No.........

Cock.......................   Hen ....
Date paired ....   1st egg laid..................
Due to hatch ....   No. of eggs..................

Date hatched	......	....	....	....	....
Ring No.	....	....	....	....	....
Colour	....	....	....	....	....
Sex	....	....	....	....	....
Remarks	....	....	....	....	....

As the breeding operations progress, the cards must be filled in and at the close of the breeding season all details transferred to the stock register. The breeding card is more or less self-explanatory, it being only necessary to explain that colour and ring number of the cock and hen and the pair number must be inserted when the birds are placed in their breeding pens. Any particular occurrence or notable good or bad habits on the part of the parents can be written at the bottom of the card and also any details regarding clear or addled eggs or dead-in-shell, etc.

A stock register can be purchased or one can be made up from an exercise book and this should contain first of all details of the whole of the stock at the commencement of the year, showing ring number, colour, sex, age, how and by whom bred or from whom purchased and any other particulars which may occur to the breeder.

The birds used for breeding should be numbered off in pairs when breeding commences and the following pages numbered off consecutively and used for inserting details of the breeding results from each pair as per the breeding cards. At the end of the season, a complete list of all the youngsters reared can be compiled, showing ring number, date hatched, colour, sex and from which pair bred. By this means a complete record of the stock is obtained which should be carried forward at the commencement of the following year.

These records are essential if the hobby is to be taken seriously and a great deal of information relating to the merits of each bird as a parent can be obtained from them. This information is exceedingly useful for breeding purposes and records should always be studied prior to pairing.

Laying and incubating. After the first egg has been laid, about eight days after mating has taken place, the succeeding eggs will be laid on alternate days and the hen may lay any number up to about seven but larger clutches are quite common. Five is the number generally met with and the eggs are normally white. They vary somewhat in shape, some hens laying quite a roundish egg whilst others are more pointed.

The hen does not always commence to sit immediately the first egg is laid, although some do, but when the second egg appears the hen sits tight until the last egg of the clutch is hatched.

The incubation period is from 17 to 19 days, but invariably the chick is hatched on the 18th day from the egg being laid, therefore as soon as the first egg appears the date should be inserted on the breeding card and 18 days added to it to give the date when the chick is due. This hatching date should also be inserted and the expected hatching watched for and noted on the card when the chick appears.

During the laying and incubation period the hen should not be disturbed more than is necessary, especially at night, although a brief inspection of the nest box may be made now and again to see that all is well and also to ascertain how many eggs have been laid. The nest box should not be cleaned out at this period; it will, in fact, be hardly necessary, although any eggs which may have become coated with excreta should be carefully cleaned by wiping with a rag damped in warm water.

The hen will come out each morning for a brief period and may visit the seed pot now and again, although the cock will see that she is kept supplied with food. If it is observed that the hen is staying out too long and there is a danger of the eggs becoming chilled, efforts should be made to induce her to return to the nest box and this she will generally do if the breeding pen or cage is closely approached.

Hatching. About the 18th day after the first egg is laid the first chick should hatch and the others will follow on more or less alternate days, always provided, of course, that the eggs are fertile. This can be ascertained to a certain extent when the egg has been laid about 10 days, a fertile egg presenting a solid, white pebbly appearance, while a clear egg, i.e., one that has not been fertilised, will still possess the clear pearly appearance as when laid.

The beginner is advised not to interfere with the eggs prior to hatching in order to ascertain whether they are fertile or not.

He is also advised to avoid disturbing the hen too much around hatching time. When the chick is due a slight tapping may be heard from within the egg and possibly also a faint chirping should the egg be held close to the ear and this is caused by the chick in its efforts to break out of the shell.

This it does by piercing the inner membrane or skin lining the egg shell and also by penetrating the shell itself with a tiny point on its beak. This point disappears after hatching but is used to cut the egg shell in half so that the chick can release itself. An egg on the point of hatching can be seen to have a line of protuberances and slight chips around the centre, caused by the chick in its efforts to break out.

During the first day after hatching, the chick will exist on the remnants of the egg yolk which it absorbs into its abdomen, but thereafter the hen will feed it from her crop and growth will be fairly rapid.

It should be borne in mind, however, that as the eggs are laid on alternate days, so will the chicks emerge. Therefore, in a clutch of five or six eggs, the first youngster will be eight or nine days old by the time the last egg is hatched and the difference in size will be considerable. The smallest youngster is liable to be deprived of its share of food or may even be squashed by its nest mates. This is where foster parents are so valuable as we shall see later.

A daily peep into the nest box at hatching time is quite enough, but remove any chick that should die, and watch for half an egg shell which may have become jammed over another egg which is still to hatch. This is quite a common occurrence and the half shell should be removed, otherwise it may have an adverse effect on the hatching of the egg over which it has become lodged.

Eggs which have failed to hatch should be examined before they are discarded as one or two may still contain a live chick which has been dilatory in emerging from the shell. Clear eggs will be obvious as also will those that are addled, i.e., the germ has died and the contents of the egg turned bad. These eggs will present a dirty yellowish appearance.

An egg which is long overdue and appears to be fertile may be found to contain a dead chick, fully developed, known as " dead-in-shell ", and eggs may also be found with the contents dried up into a hard lump, caused by the egg shell being punctured and the air admitted. These hatching failures will be dealt with in a later chapter.

A chick which is experiencing difficulty in breaking out of the shell may be assisted up to a point but beyond that point it is best to leave matters to take their own course. Sometimes when the hatching is overdue, the chick may still be heard piping away within the egg and in this case the egg should be gently rubbed all round with a well moistened forefinger when the tip of the beak will be plainly felt underlying the shell.

Rub this point carefully, keeping the finger well moistened, and this will have the effect of assisting the tip of the beak to break through the shell. The egg should then be replaced in the nest box. The practice in such cases of chipping the shell in order to help the chick out is one I do not recommend as I have experienced varying results. In some instances all has gone well, the chick emerging and living, whilst in others the chick has either failed to break out completely and has died or has freed itself of the shell but has died soon afterwards.

The danger lies in the fact that during the incubation period the chick is attached to the inner membrane of the egg shell and normally a separation occurs when the chick is ready to break out, but when the shell is chipped in order to assist matters, the chick may emerge before the inside of the shell has been cleared up and this premature hatching is fatal.

Several methods are used as an aid to hatching, but with healthy stock, efficient housing and normal weather conditions such aids are unnecessary. Some breeders sprinkle or lightly spray the eggs in the nest box with warm water a day or so prior to hatching but I do not recommend this procedure as, apart from tending to make the nest box messy, there is the possibility of an egg becoming sticky with excreta in the box and adhering to the hen and being carried out the next time she leaves the nest.

The egg will then drop on to the floor and if remaining intact will become chilled and useless. I have actually witnessed such an occurrence, the egg adhering to the hen just below the vent and she was able to carry it out from the box without it being knocked off by the sides of the entrance hole.

If the eggs are wiped dry after sprinkling this defeats the object of the treatment which is to create humid conditions so that the inner membrane of the egg shell will not dry and toughen, and so make it difficult for the chick to break through.

Another method is to float the eggs in warm water round about hatching time and those containing live chicks will be seen to bob about quite vigorously. This procedure is also designed to soften the inner membrane of the egg shell but here again the same disadvantage is present as in the former method.

A word of warning regarding the floating of eggs in warm water. Great care must be taken not wholly to *immerse* the eggs, otherwise, the egg shell being porous, the air in the air space at the broad end of the egg will be driven out and the chick within will die.

Ringing. For purposes of identification and record, all young Budgerigars should be rung with a numbered ring. Should the breeder be a member of the Budgerigar Society or an Area Society a code number will be allocated and this will consist of the initial letter of the breeder's surname followed by a number.

These rings are of aluminium of a different colour for each year and are closed, i.e., without a break in them. During the last war, coloured aluminium rings were unobtainable and plain metal had to be used. The rings bear the breeder's code number, the last two numbers of the year and are numbered consecutively.

Split rings, i.e., not a complete unbroken circle, are also obtainable, both in aluminium and in celluloid, but these are not recognised by the Budgerigar Society as they can be placed on the bird's leg at any age and are no proof that the bird wearing such a ring was bred by the exhibitor. A bird that does not wear a closed, coded ring is not eligible to compete in breeders' classes at any shows patronised by the Budgerigar Society, or by any of its affiliated Area Societies.

Should the breeder not be a member of the Budgerigar or Area Society, closed aluminium rings can still be obtained but these will bear the breeder's initials instead of a code number. Closed celluloid rings are also available in various colours.

As a proof of breeding, as well as from a recording point of view, young Budgerigars should always be rung with a closed ring at the age of from six to eight days but the actual time will be governed by the development of the chick. It is better to ring too early and risk the ring coming off into the nest box than to leave it too late and then find that the ring will not go on. Should the ring come off, it must be found and replaced, when it will probably remain in position.

There is no difficulty in close ringing a Budgerigar, although many beginners seem rather apprehensive when attempting the operation. The chick should be held in the left hand and the leg grasped between thumb and forefinger at the joint above the foot with the claws projecting out beyond the tips of the thumb and forefinger. It will be seen that there are two long claws, one a little shorter and another considerably smaller still.

Take the ring between the thumb and the forefinger of the right hand with the ring number so that it can be read when the bird is

Three stages in ringing a young Budgerigar

standing upright and slip the ring over the two longest claws. Next work the ring gently along so that the remaining two claws are laid back under the ring alongside the leg when it will be found that the ring is prevented from going any farther by the knuckle joint whilst the claws are held against the leg by the ring. These two claws must then be gently pulled through the ring by means of a sharpened matchstick and the ringing operation is complete.

See that the ring is left just above the claws and is not inadvertently pushed up above the " elbow ". Should this occur and remain unnoticed until the bird has considerably developed, suffering will occur and the ring may have to be cut off, should it prove impossible, with the aid of Vaseline, to ease it down over the joint to its proper position.

The accompanying drawings show the procedure to be adopted and the ring number must, of course, be recorded on the breeding card. Should the operation of ringing be left a little late and difficulty experienced in getting the ring over the claws, a little Vaseline smeared over the foot will facilitate matters.

Another method of ringing is to slip the ring over the *three* largest claws and then pull the small claw through the ring as in the former method which I prefer and always adopt. In a well developed chick the bunching together of three claws presents quite an obstruction to the ring and apart from rendering the operation of ringing more difficult, may be the cause of pain or injury being inflicted on the youngsters.

Split rings can be placed on a bird at any age and split celluloid rings of various colours are very useful for marking birds for varying purposes and can be used to denote parentage in the following manner. When a pair is placed in the breeding pen, both birds can be rung with the same coloured split celluloid ring which is usually placed on the leg which does not carry the closed ring.

All the youngsters from the mating are rung with the same coloured split ring as well as with a closed ring and by this means, when a number of birds of the same colour are flying together in the aviary, parentage or relationship can be ascertained at a glance without the necessity of catching them up. This is particularly useful with largish stocks where it is impossible to memorise the pedigree of the bird. The coloured rings need not be placed on the youngsters until they are about to leave the nest.

Split rings are placed in position by means of a special ringing tool which is supplied by the makers when this type of ring is ordered and full instructions are also provided, therefore there is no necessity to describe the procedure here beyond remarking that the operation is extremely simple.

Foster parents. The use of foster parents can now be described and as previously stated it is most useful to put up one or two pairs for this purpose when the breeding pairs are mated.

They should be allowed to lay their clutch of eggs, the hatching date of which will more or less correspond to that of the eggs from the breeding pairs. Should one or more of these pairs be of particular value and the breeder not wish to subject them to the strain of rearing a family, their eggs, when the full clutch has been laid, can be transferred to the foster parents, whose eggs will, of course, have to be destroyed. Any difference in the number of eggs is quite immaterial.

The foster parents will hatch out the eggs and rear the chicks as if they were their own and the high quality parent birds can be replaced in the flights unless it is desired to obtain another clutch from them; if this is the case these eggs can also be placed under another pair of foster parents. The same procedure can be adopted if it is known that one or other of the breeding pair is an unsatisfactory parent but at the same time it is desired to obtain young from them.

Even if it is not desired to use foster parents for either of the above reasons, they should still be utilised to take over youngsters from overcrowded nests and in this case they should be allowed to hatch their own eggs and their chicks would be replaced by the surplus youngsters from the breeding pairs.

No pair should be allowed to rear more than four chicks per nest but there is no necessity to destroy any above that number. After all the chicks in any overcrowded nest have been safely rung, four can be left for the parent birds to rear and the remainder transferred to the foster parents and if this should have the effect of overcrowding that particular nest, the chicks from the foster parents can either be destroyed or distributed among other nests.

This distribution of chicks among various nests can be performed without the aid of foster parents, provided it does not result in any pair having to rear more than four youngsters. Care should be taken to see that there is not a big discrepancy in the size of the youngsters, as obviously a six days' old chick would stand little chance of being successfully reared in a nest with three others each about three weeks old.

Make sure, therefore, that when chicks are distributed around various nest boxes they are placed with others of about the same size, and also, if it should be necessary to destroy all the young from foster parents in order to make room for others from overcrowded nests, see that they are replaced by chicks of about the same age as those destroyed. Budgerigars, being extremely accommodating in this direction, do not appear to show any resentment when their youngsters are switched about.

They do not seem to mind how much the youngsters are added to or subtracted from and certainly do not appear to know their own chicks before they are feathered. If they do, they show little concern when one is taken from the nest box or if a stranger is added.

For accuracy in recording, it is best not to make any changes until the youngsters have been rung. Should there be a clutch of six or seven eggs in one nest box, they can all be left to hatch and then the first hatched chick transferred either to foster parents or to another nest after it has been rung and this procedure can be followed with successive chicks, leaving the last four for the actual parents to rear.

In short, it is possible and quite safe to re-arrange nests with or without the aid of foster parents in such a manner that each pair has to rear a maximum of four chicks only and in this way the parents are not subjected to an undue strain and each youngster has a good chance of survival.

Some breeders carry the process even farther by re-arranging nests, even if they are not overcrowded, in such a manner that each nest contains chicks all about the same size. This is done, for instance, in two nests, each containing four chicks, the hatching date of the eggs in each nest more or less coinciding. Each nest would contain four chicks, the largest being about six or seven days older than the last hatched and an exchange would be made of the two largest chicks in one nest for the two smallest in the other, resulting in each nest then containing chicks of more or less the same size and age.

This procedure is quite permissible and does more or less ensure that each youngster receives its fair share of food and so develops normally, there being no large brothers or sisters to clamour for more than their portion.

Nest-box hygiene. As previously stated, it is not advisable to interfere too frequently with the nest box during laying, incubation and hatching, but an inspection must be made at intervals and during the rearing period this should be made daily as once all the eggs have been hatched the nest box will tend to become foul with wasted regurgitated food and with droppings from the growing chicks.

The nest box should have been quite clean when first placed in the breeding pen and it will generally be found that the hen will keep it so up to the time the chicks are hatched, but from then onwards it is up to the breeder to see that the chicks are reared under the cleanest possible conditions, otherwise trouble in various ways will probably be experienced.

A sprinkling of clean pine sawdust or fine peat moss litter will do much towards absorbing the droppings and will help to avoid sourness, but all masses of excreta and wasted food should first be removed and as the chicks increase in size it may be found necessary to replace the loose concave bottom with a clean one, but see that the replacement is not damp or too cold or the chicks may contract a chill.

The youngsters can be placed in any suitable receptacle such as a small cardboard box placed on the floor of the breeding pen for the few moments which it takes to replace the dirty concave with a clean one, which should receive its sprinkling of sawdust or peat moss litter when it has been placed in position in the nest box. On replacing the youngsters the hen will invariably enter the box immediately to see that all is well.

Some hens are dirty feeders and smother the inside of the nest box and sometimes the chicks as well with regurgitated food, whilst others are models of daintiness and are free from such an undesirable habit. The cleaner the nest box is kept, the less likelihood there will be of subsequent trouble with the chicks in the form of stuck up claws and feathers, etc. Furthermore, in a dirty, sour nest box, the possibility of disease arising must be greater than in a nest which is kept clean and wholesome.

Concave bottoms can easily be cleaned by first scraping well with the edge of an old spoon and then, after soaking in boiling soda water, scrubbing hard with a stiff bristled brush, rinsing in boiling water, draining and left to dry. This treatment effectively removes all traces of excreta and dried waste food and results in as hygienically clean a concave as possible.

Care of young chicks. As the chicks develop in size, so must they be examined daily to see that all is progressing satisfactorily, the main points for observation being beak, feet and vent.

See that the beak and nostrils are kept free from caked, regurgitated food and examine particularly the inside of the upper mandible where sometimes a portion of dried food becomes lodged. This should carefully be removed with a pointed matchstick as, if allowed to remain, an undershot beak will most probably develop. This takes the form of the lower mandible growing over the upper and the bird is useless for all practical purposes.

If it should be found that despite every attention an undershot beak appears to be developing, a cure can generally be effected by trimming off very carefully the tip of the *upper* mandible with a pair of sharp nail scissors. Only the extreme end of the beak should be severed and care must be taken not to cut too far up the beak and draw blood. In most cases it will be found that thereafter the upper mandible will grow normally over the lower, but should the treatment not be success-ful, the bird should be destroyed.

The beak does not become really hard until the bird is some weeks old, therefore it is obvious that it is essential to keep it free from caked and dried food which, if allowed to remain, will interfere with the development of the beak and may even cause malformation. An undershot beak does not generally make itself evident until the chick is about 3–4 weeks old.

The feet also should receive careful attention, particularly in cases where the hen is a somewhat dirty feeder. If the nest box is allowed to become dirty, food and excreta will cake round the youngsters' claws and will harden into a solid ball, sometimes difficult to remove.

If this will not come off easily, the feet should be moistened with warm water to soften the caked substance which can then easily be removed, but care must be taken to see that the toe-nails are not removed with it. These will, in a young chick, come out fairly easily and the bird will be spoilt for exhibition as the toe-nails will not grow again. Therefore use every care in removing caked matter from the feet.

The vent and tail stub must also be kept free from sticky or caked food and excreta, and here again care must be exercised in its removal or growing tail feathers will come with it. Never hesitate to use warm water to soften any caked up material which may adhere to the chicks' beak, feet or vent, it's a little more trouble but it's safer.

Sometimes a young chick is found with its crop distended. This may be caused by careless feeding on the part of the hen, by the chick's nostrils being clogged with dried food, or by the food itself in the chick's crop fermenting and producing gases which blow out the crop.

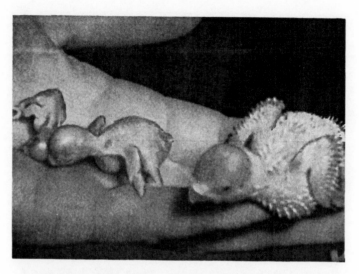

Budgerigar chicks from the same nest, two, four, and eight days old

In this picture of three young Budgies the difference can be clearly seen between a Normal (left), Lutino and an Opaline (right)

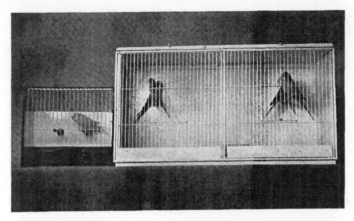

Budgerigars in training. A hole in the large cage coincides with the show cage door enabling the birds to be moved from one to the other

An exhibition specimen in a standard Budgerigar show cage. The overall measurements of the cage are 14in. long, 12in. high and 6½in. wide

Whatever the cause, the condition may be serious and calls for immediate attention, otherwise the chick may die.

If the nostrils are found to be obstructed, they must very carefully be freed of the caked food and an attempt made to expel the wind from the crop.

This can usually be done by gently squeezing the crop, when the gases and sour liquid will be expelled through the beak. Do not be hesitant in this operation, but squeeze the crop gently but firmly towards the beak, and although such a procedure may seem rather drastic, in practice it is very effective and usually no harm results.

Observation must also be kept on the feeding capacities of the hen. Some hens are excellent feeders and keep the chicks well supplied with food, but now and again a poor feeder is met with, the hen being dilatory in this respect and paying more attention to the cock than she does to her youngsters. Should it be found that the chicks are but meagrely fed, as will be evidenced by empty crops, the chicks will be slow in developing, and should be fostered out to more reliable parents.

Two further setbacks to successful breeding are sometimes encountered and these are feather plucking and French Moult. In the former, the young chicks are partially or completely stripped of their feathers on the head, neck, back and wing butts by the hen and if this should occur the chicks should be fostered out or, if this is not possible, the hen should be removed and the cock allowed to continue rearing by himself. Feather plucking will be dealt with more fully in the following chapter on Breeding Setbacks.

French Moult is characterised by a sudden dropping of the flights and sometimes also of the secondary and tail feathers when the chicks are three to four weeks old. The feathers will be found in the nest box, and will be seen to be rotted where they have broken away at the base of the feather shaft, and the feather vanes will sometimes be curled or wavy. Further comments on this trouble will be found in a later chapter dealing with Common Ailments.

Should a cock unfortunately die whilst youngsters are being reared, the hen will invariably carry on with their upbringing on her own, but should the hen expire and the youngsters be still surviving when the hen is discovered dead, the young should be fostered out, although in many instances the cock will continue to feed them. If the hen should die whilst still incubating, the eggs will in all probability be cold and useless, but if still warm they can be placed under other hens, preferably of a different colour from the original pair, in order that identification of the chicks may be possible later.

It must not be thought from a perusal of the foregoing that the path of the Budgerigar breeder is beset with pitfalls or that every nest carries its brood of trouble. With healthy stock, correct feeding and management the reverse is the rule, and usually young Budgerigars develop rapidly from the time they are hatched until they leave the nest box at about four to five weeks old, fully feathered and able to fly.

At this stage they are not often able to feed themselves, although some precocious youngsters will crack seed immediately they leave the nest box. The youngsters must be left with their parents until they can assimilate a sufficient amount of food by their own efforts to sustain themselves, and although the cock will continue to feed them as well as the hen whilst she is laying her second clutch, a careful watch should be kept and as soon as the youngsters are seen to be cracking seed quite freely, generally about a week to 10 days after emerging from the nest box, they should be removed to their training quarters, and the adults left to carry on with their next round of youngsters if it is so desired.

Whilst the young Budgerigars are still with their parents and learning to feed, they are liable to get into mischief as youngsters of all species will, and a careful watch must be kept to see that they come to no harm.

Youngsters are also prone to clambering in and out of the water pot and care should be taken to see that they do not roost whilst still very wet or chills may develop, especially if exposed to draughts. A young Budgerigar so saturated should be caged up and placed in a warm spot, i.e., in front of a fire, to dry off and then returned to its parents.

Sometimes a youngster will clamber out of the nest box before it is fully feathered and will be unable to find its way back. In such cases the bird should be replaced in the nest box, otherwise the possibility of the sparsely feathered chick contracting a chill certainly exists.

See that an ample supply of good seed, with cuttle-fish bone, suitable grit, fresh water and greenstuff in moderation is always available whilst breeding is in progress, and do not neglect the supplementary diet as described in Chapter 3.

Characteristics of the young Budgerigar. The development from the naked chick stage through the growing period when first the fluffy down appears and then the tiny feathers from which the colour of the chick is established is a period full of interest, culminating in the emergence from the nest box of the baby Budgerigar clad in its soft toned feathers.

The nest-feather Budgerigar differs in appearance from the adult of the same colour inasmuch as in addition to the colours being softer than in the adult stage, wing markings are less distinct and the throat spots are present in a different form. These, in the youngster, take the shape of flecking across the base of the mask and, as a general rule, the larger and more dense the flecking, the larger the subsequent throat spots will be.

These appear at the first moult when the young Budgerigar assumes its adult plumage, the tiny feathers carrying the flecking being dropped and replaced by others bearing the throat spots. With the assumption of adult plumage the body colour deepens and wing markings become more clear cut.

The head of a young Budgerigar of the Green and Blue series also differs from that of the adult. Across the forehead and across as far down as the nape of the neck, bars of markings are present in a youngster, such birds being referred to as barred-headed. These markings disappear from the forehead with the first moult and are replaced by clear feathers, which, with a mask of the same colour, form the characteristic head of the adult Budgerigar.

The sex of a youngster is not always easy to determine, as the characteristic deep blue cere of the cock and the rich brown cere of the hen are not always discernible, the cere of a youngster usually being of an indeterminate flesh colour. As a general rule, the cere of a young cock when first out of the nest box is a deep pink, deepening further within a week or so to blue, whilst a hen can generally be determined by the bluish colour of the cere with a whitish edge to the nostrils, the cere deepening to a pale brown after a few weeks. Once a Budgerigar has assumed its adult plumage, it is not possible to determine its age by any means other than the leg ring. Young Lutinos and Albinos are particularly difficult for the beginner to sex correctly.

The second round. When the first round youngsters leave the nest box, and sometimes before the last one or two have ventured into the outside world, the hen will commence to lay her second clutch of eggs, and the whole procedure of laying, incubating, etc., is repeated. The first one or two eggs will in all probability become fouled with excreta if any of the first round youngsters are still in the box, so take pains at this stage to keep the nest box as clean as possible. When the last of the youngsters has left, slip in a clean concave and gently replace the eggs. From then onwards treat the breeding pair in exactly the same manner as during the first round.

Make sure that the birds are in a fit condition to carry on breeding. If either of them shows signs of not being quite fit, it is safer to remove the nest box in order that they will not have to undergo the strain of rearing a further nest of chicks. It is this process that imposes the strain, not that of egg laying, therefore never allow them to continue breeding if they appear to be below par.

As a general rule, chicks from subsequent rounds are not quite so good as those from the first round, but this must not be accepted as a hard and fast fact, as " stormers " *are* bred in the second round, but as the parents have already undergone a month of intensive effort necessitated by the rearing of one batch of youngsters, it is only reasonable to assume that any further efforts required in this direction will not be quite so effective as in the first instance.

It is unwise to allow any pair to rear more than eight or nine youngsters per season. If allowed to bring up more than this number (which can be spread over two or three rounds), their stamina will undoubtedly suffer and the following year's breeding results may be disappointing.

Budgerigars will continue to rear clutch after clutch so long as the nest box is left in position, but if allowed to do so they would probably die through exhaustion, therefore call a halt after a reasonable number of chicks has been reared.

When it is decided to bring the breeding activities of a pair to a close and the last of the youngsters has left the nest, the nest box should be removed, but the parents allowed to stay with their youngsters until the breeder is quite certain that they can all fend for themselves. When this stage is reached, the parents should be replaced in their usual quarters and the nest box and concave well scoured with boiling soda water, allowed to dry and put away for the following season. The breeding cage or pen should be similarly cleaned out and renovated if necessary ready for future breeding activities.

BREEDING SETBACKS

WITH proper feeding and management, healthy stock gives little trouble during the breeding season, the majority of the pairs conducting their domestic activities from start to finish with the minimum of interference, but setbacks do occur, however, and those most commonly met with are as follows:—

Failure of hen to go to nest. Due in most cases to the hen not being in breeding condition, showing the breeder's judgment has been at fault when putting up pairs for breeding. May also be due to minor causes such as antipathy towards the cock or a dislike of the nest-box situation. As an example, I once put up a pair in a breeding cage with an inside nest box, the nearest perch to which was about 1ft. away. The birds appeared to be in breeding condition, but the hen refused to enter the nest box until I moved the perch an inch or so nearer, whereon she immediately flew on to the perch and from thence into the box and thereafter laid her clutch.

Another cause of failure to nest may be that the size of the entrance hole to the nest box is too small or too large.

A diameter of about 1½in. is usually satisfactory, and although hens in breeding condition will usually gnaw their way into the nest box through a hole that is too small, they may not always do so, and will sometimes sit disconsolate on the nest-box perch and make no effort to obtain admittance to the box.

A hen will sometimes refuse to enter a nest box with too large an entrance hole, either because the interior of the box is thus not sufficiently private or because of a possible inherent fear that a larger bird or animal may gain access to the nest and wreak destruction therein.

If the hen fails to go to nest and there is nothing in the foregoing to explain her reticence, all that can be done is to replace her in the aviary and wait a week or so until she does come into condition.

Eggs or chicks thrown out of the nest box. Cause uncertain. May be due to the presence of mice at night, sudden lights or other nocturnal disturbance. Sometimes experienced with an old or a nervous hen or with a hen disinclined to take her maternal duties seriously. It *is* possible for eggs or chicks to be accidentally carried out of the box by the hen, the egg adhering to feathers round the vent or to tail feathers the bases of which have become soiled with excreta.

It is probable that some cases of eggs or chicks being found on the floor of the breeding pen are due to accident and not to design.

Clear eggs. May be due to one of several causes. Incomplete mating due to loose and partially revolving perches, failure to mate at all through the cock not being in breeding condition, sterility in the hen or in much rarer cases, in the cock, will all cause clear eggs to be laid. Make sure that all perches are fixed firmly and that the cock is in breeding condition.

Addled eggs. These are eggs in which the germ has commenced to develop but has died from some cause, the egg turning bad. Eggs which have become cold through the hen remaining off them too long will addle, and an occasional bad egg need cause no concern, but should they be numerous from any particular pair, this would point to debility or disease in one or in both of the birds.

It is easy to determine this by breaking up the pair and re-mating each with a different partner, and should addled eggs appear from one of the new pairs, the bird responsible is located.

Egg-binding. This troublesome complaint is seldom met with if the hens are allowed plenty of exercise during the non-breeding season and they are not used for breeding when too young or when not in breeding condition.

An attack may occur at any time during the laying period, either in the first or in subsequent rounds. The hen will, in the first stage, be found out of the nest box, generally on a perch looking ruffled and thick, very troubled and the picture of discomfort. Should she fail to soon pass the egg, the condition will worsen and she will probably be found on the floor with wings slightly outspread, rump somewhat erected and tail well down with the area round the vent very red and swollen. The condition is now serious and unless immediate steps are taken to remove the egg, the hen will most certainly die.

As soon as a hen is observed to be in trouble, and this is easily discernible by her absence from the nest box (in rarer cases she may be found lying on her side in the box), she should immediately be removed to a hospital cage with temperature 90–100 degrees.

If a hospital cage is not available, any smallish box cage will do, and this should be placed in front of a fire or over a stove in a draught-proof position. *Warmth* is the essential part of the treatment, with a constant temperature maintained day and night if possible. Warm olive oil should be administered to the vent by means of a feather, whereon the more or less convulsive, straining efforts of the hen to expel the egg will work the oil upwards into the passage.

In normal cases, the egg should be expelled within a few hours, but if this does not occur and the condition of the bird worsens, an effort must be made to remove the egg. This is most definitely *not* an operation for a novice to attempt. The assistance of an experienced Fancier must be sought, and the procedure is to very gently exert a little pressure with the thumb *behind* the egg so as to force it towards the vent, applying warm olive oil each time the egg passage is exposed by the pressure.

A tiny white spot will eventually appear in the passage thus exposed and this is the first sign of the egg, appearing through the aperture in the oviduct. Repeated pressure and warm olive oil will eventually cause the egg to be expelled into the hand, but the bird will be very exhausted and must, under no conditions, be replaced in the breeding pen. She should be kept in the warm for a day or so and given a tonic such as Parrish's Chemical Food in the drinking water or one or two drops of whisky may be used, diluted with a similar quantity of water and given through the beak by means of a fountain pen filler.

The procedure described is definitely a " kill or cure " operation, and should the egg be broken inside the bird, this will be fatal, and even if the egg is successfully removed, it does not follow that the bird will recover from the strain, but should a bad case of egg-binding be met with, I certainly advise the breeder to seek assistance if he does not feel capable of performing the operation, because unless the egg is expelled either naturally or by operation, the bird will die.

See that hens used for breeding are not over fat, as this can be a cause of egg-binding, as also can general debility; therefore, make sure that hens are fit in every respect before being given a mate.

An internal injury, such as a laceration which may have occurred during previous laying, may also be the cause of egg-binding.

Do not forget the cod liver oil food prior to breeding and never, under any circumstances, use a bird that has been egg-bound, until the following season for breeding again.

Dead-in-shell. These chicks, fully formed but failing to break out of the shell through one of several reasons, may be found within the egg shell after hatching is long overdue.

When the egg is broken, the interior will sometimes be found to be very dry, denoting that in all probability undue dryness of the atmosphere has toughened the inner membrane of the shell and the chick has been unable to break through. Such a chick would probably not have been very robust had it hatched successfully.

A chick may die within a day or so previous to hatching time either through general debility or disease inherited from the parents or the hen may have allowed the egg to become chilled. Undue dryness of the atmosphere, especially during periods when a drying, easterly wind is prevailing, is difficult to counteract; therefore, the great thing is to keep the stock in the pink of condition so that only robust chicks are produced and avoid excess heat and consequent dryness in the birdroom.

Another cause of dead-in-shell is abnormal thickness of the egg shell due to a maladjustment of the shell-forming mechanism in the hen. The egg is enveloped with an excess of lime, forming in some cases a shell through which it is impossible for any normal chick to penetrate. Such cases are not usual.

Failure of hen to feed chicks. Sometimes met with in young hens and is probably due to nervousness or inexperience. Foster out the chicks if still alive and allow the hen to lay another clutch. She will probably feed the next lot of youngsters quite well. As a precaution, always mate a maiden hen with a two or three year old cock.

Feather plucking. Opinions are divided as to the cause of this most exasperating habit on the part of some hens. Promising youngsters of about three to four weeks old are deprived of their feathers from head, neck, back and sometimes even from the wings and a chick so plucked presents a sorry appearance. The feathers will grow again in time, but this in itself throws a strain on the chick and known feather pluckers should not be used for breeding unless the young are fostered out.

One cannot be too dogmatic regarding the cause of this annoying habit. It has not been proved to be hereditary and it may be due to boredom, to sheer mischievousness, to a desire to be rid of the youngsters and lay a fresh clutch, or it may even be due to a deficiency of some kind in the diet. Once a hen commences the habit of feather plucking, she never loses it; therefore chicks from a known feather plucker should either be fostered out to more reliable parents with young of about the same size or the hen should be removed and the cock allowed to rear the young by himself. The parents must not be paired again until these young have been weaned.

Eggs dried up. Sometimes when an egg has failed to hatch and it has been opened it is found to contain a small dried up, pea-like substance, rolling about loose inside the shell. This is a case where the egg shell has been punctured by the claws of one of the parents and the contents of the shell have dried up through air being admitted. The puncture may be too small to see easily but the tiniest hole will be sufficient to cause drying. Second round eggs are sometimes punctured by the first round chicks which may still be within the nest box.

In order to lessen the possibility of punctured eggs, examine the claws of the adult birds before pairing, and if they are found to be abnormally long and sharp, they should be carefully trimmed with a pair of nail scissors, the tip of the claw and no more, being taken off.

Broken eggs. In cases where Budgerigar eggs are broken, the usual cause can be attributed to a cock that spends a good deal of time in the nest box. He either breaks the eggs through sheer curiosity or so unsettles the hen that they are broken during subsequent scuffling. The shells are usually eaten and the contents disseminated by the birds' feet, the trouble most often being encountered with young birds.

All that can be done in such cases is to allow the hen to lay again and remove the cock after the next two eggs appear in the hope that all of the clutch will have been fertilised. The hen can be left to incubate and rear the young by herself, but the cock must not be allowed in with her again until all the chicks have been weaned and removed from her.

BREEDING

How excited we are when the first egg is laid, and with what impatience we await the hatching !

The breeding season is from April until August, and it is during this period that we must follow nature closely if we are to establish a strong strain of Budgerigars.

I am, and always shall be, strongly opposed to winter breeding. Before giving my reasons for this statement I must show fairness to the advocates of winter breeding by admitting that there are certain advantages to be gained through breeding during the winter months, and whether such advantages are worth while must be left to my readers. Some birds may not come into condition during the summer, and advantage can be taken of this by their owners during the " off " season should they show form. The only circumstances warranting such procedure are artificial conditions of lighting and heating. I am prepared to admit also that winter-bred young will be fully moulted before the early exhibitions, and will not be called upon to withstand the injurious effects of changeable weather, damp or cold, whilst completing the moult.

Nature and Balance

Conditions of wild life when not interfered with by man are a matter of balance. Nature holds the scales and provides the antidote for a too generous provision of any one species or of any particular type. Nature also sees to it that in so doing the surplus is not wasted, but is turned to account in providing for and supporting some other form of life.

When man, however, for his own ends interferes with the primeval conditions, the balance is disturbed, and unless adequate precautions are taken full benefit is not gained from the animal which it is desired to cultivate, to improve and increase.

Very well, then. To breed wild birds successfully in captivity we must follow Nature. Wild birds separate during the winter and chaffinches are never seen together in pairs during this period.

That Nature will avenge any abuse is proved by the rickety young obtained in the second generation from winter-bred birds, proving clearly that " the sins of the parents are visited upon the children ".

No bird is more subject to changes of temperature than the Budgerigar, and we have this fact to contend with during the winter. Artificial conditions can never remedy this state of affairs.

Then we have the long dark nights. I am prepared for the argument that parents feed their babies during the night, but this does not provide sufficient sustenance as the parents are unable to replenish their own crops during this period.

In few aviaries during the winter will the young leave their nest at the usual period.

Further trouble arises when they do so. They cannot feed themselves during this period of darkness, and, at the most critical period of their existence have to withstand sudden changes of temperature, which militates against any advantage gained later, and to which I have referred previously.

I dismiss the fact that the Australian summer coincides with our winter, as the Budgerigar is now an acclimatized bird.

The lack of sunshine and food vitamin content, and their natural food (grasses) are further proof if necessary.

These, then, are my reasons for dating the breeding season for the spring or summer.

I must refer, first, to the breeding in cages. Personally I have never had any success with this method. Being gregarious, a single pair of Budgerigars will seldom attempt to nest, unless either another pair of birds are introduced, or a pair are placed in another cage near at hand, so that the birds can see each other.. I am aware that many well-known breeders have been more lucky than I.

The great advantage of using a cage is that we have absolute control over the birds, and can dismiss any suggestions of infidelity. We can also dismiss the risk of fighting.

Lack of exercise and consequent egg-binding are drawbacks to breeding in cages, and if cages are used the parents should be caged only when breeding has begun, and liberated in the aviary as soon as the second-round young are weaned. The young, too, should be put out the moment they can fend for themselves.

Whilst cock Budgerigars are generally friendly, and we can even chance an odd cock in an aviary, we can on no account run the risk of an odd hen. Hens are not so amiable when breeding ; two or more usually fancy the same nest box, and if many birds are kept together, murder will result. This is the great drawback to colony breeding.

In a wild state, Budgerigars seem to manifest a tendency to pair for life. Bearing this fact in mind we can take advantage of it by pairing first in cages before admitting to an aviary for breeding purposes.

The Ideal Method of Breeding

The ideal method of breeding is to keep only a few pairs in the same aviary, and allowing many nest boxes, which should be placed facing the light, at the same height, and in as much the same position as possible so as to allow little choice of position. By keeping few birds, in long narrow compartments, we shall obtain more young than by keeping double the quantity in flocks.

It is necessary to digress at this point, and discuss the infidelity of the Budgerigar under conditions of domestication. This is notorious. In breeding the different colour varieties we shall not obtain our expectations if all colours are mixed up, and can give no guarantee of parentage.

A suggestion to mitigate this difficulty is to keep only cocks of one colour in certain departments. For instance, Aviary No. 1 will contain only blue cocks, and Aviary No. 2 white cocks. We can then be certain that any young in

No. 1 aviary had a blue as their father, and the young in No. 2 a white father.

I have also to call attention, before proceeding, to two fallacies that exist. The first is that a hen eats her eggs, and the second that she murders her young. Whilst admitting the possibilities of both, they are very uncommon, and have seldom come under my observation. The first trouble is caused by a marauding hen entering the nest box, and the fight which ensues cracks or breaks the eggs. The hen Budgie is both an intelligent and clean bird, and will promptly remove such broken eggs with her beak, often being caught in the act. It is also such roving hens who destroy the young, wishing to obtain this particular nesting receptacle. I have seen, many times, only tiny parts of young birds remaining, the whole clutch being bitten to small fragments.

Separation is Unnecessary

I have never found our pets attempt to breed if no nesting receptacle is in the cage or aviary, neither have I found eggs deposited upon the floor during such period. It is not, then, necessary to separate the sexes during the winter months, or during such period that we have no wish to breed.

During the winter of 1932-33 I received many complaints of eggs being laid during the " off " season, after the removal of the nest boxes. As the complaints covered every system of caging and housing, and the average was highest from single hens in cages, there appears to be no clue as to the cause, and it is impossible to suggest a remedy. This unfortunate experience may have been due to climatic or other conditions over which we had no control.

Avoid Pairing Young Hens

Young hens should not be paired until fully twelve months old, and I never mate mine until June. Incidentally, Budgerigars will breed all the year round if allowed to do so, but the result will be seen in weakened constitutions, and the production of delicate young.

It is advisable to keep a record of all stock and young hatched, so that we can prevent inbreeding and provide a reliable pedigree with any birds that we may dispose of. *Cage Birds* publishes a most excellent Breeding Room Register specially drawn up for Budgerigar breeding, and apart from the well-known Canary Register issued by the paper.

To distinguish our young after they leave

the nest, all babies should be ringed whilst in the boxes with aluminium rings, which may be obtained either closed or split. Whilst closed rings guarantee the age of a bird and find favour with many breeders, they have certain disadvantages. It is necessary to slip these rings on a young bird before the feet are too large. This procedure necessitates watching the nests carefully daily, and, owing to the young hatching in relays, they need constant supervision. I have also found parents attempt to remove rings upon such young birds, and often bite their legs off.

The split ring is placed in position with a pair of special pliers provided. Coloured celluloid rings are also useful to distinguish birds flying in an aviary at a glance. I use the similar self-coloured rings for each pair of birds and a mixed colour for their young. These coloured rings save catching up all our birds to discover their number. Coloured celluloid rings should be additional to the aluminium variety, as they are often removed by the birds, and may need replacing constantly. It is now possible to obtain closed aluminium rings in various colours for identification purposes. Celluloid rings would then be unnecessary.

Reference must be made as to how long a Budgerigar will remain productive. As regards cocks, I have myself bred strong young from a bird in his thirteenth year, and kept his young successfully for stock. A well-known breeder bought this bird from me, knowing his age, and wrote me a letter the following year saying that he had again produced many fine young, paired to a young hen.

I cannot relate a similar experience with regard to hens, neither can I obtain information of any long periods of fertility from any of my friends. I have, however, heard of a hen living to be ten years old. I discovered when quite a boy that the young from a hen in her fourth season showed signs of deterioration, and the babies were few and delicate. This was no isolated case. An old hen will often make a useful foster-mother, by the way.

How to Judge Age

The question arises constantly as to how the tyro can judge the age of a bird when buying from strangers. There are no hard and fast rules by which the age of a bird can be reckoned. Some old birds appear quite fit until they break down suddenly from old age. One can only examine the legs for scales and look for soft plumage, obesity, or humped backs. These sypmtoms are not infallible, but are danger signals in any bird. If a bird is tight feathered, lively and bright eyed, there is not usually much amiss.

Provided a young hen is allowed to develop fully, and is twelve months old before pairing, and if she shows no symptoms of egg-binding, she may be regarded as at her zenith, and will produce finer young than at any period of her existence. The next best period is the second season. After this hens deteriorate rapidly. It is advisable, if fine young are desired, to dispose of all hens after their third season.

Artificial Feeding

Should valuable parents neglect their young, Konsul-General Cremer, a great authority upon Budgerigars, recommends the feeding of young in the evening by artificial methods. He uses a special syringe for this purpose. Herr Cremer has also found the addition of " Vigantol " (a proprietary form of Ergosterol), a useful addition to the food. A good mixture is made by well boiling fine oatmeal, and adding, when cooked, equal parts of Osborne biscuit. This should be administered in a tepid condition and may be sprinkled advantageously with a small quantity of finely grated cuttlefish bone.

Nature again advises us, and I follow the practice of wild birds by allowing only two nests annually, and only permitting at the most four young to be reared in each clutch.

All preparations being made and the season being well advanced, we have only to hang up our nest boxes. Supply at least two to each pair of birds, and hang about 5 ft. 6 in. high.

Nest boxes are legion. The coconut husk was at one time used universally. This was both unhygienic and awkward to inspect, and has given way to the use of wooden boxes. There are many splendid types upon the market for the breeder to select from, and it would be unfair for me to single out any special make as the best. They should be of ample size, and have a concave bottom to prevent the eggs being scattered, as the hen does not build a nest or use any material.

An average sized box should measure 9 in. in height by 4½ to 5 inches in breadth and length. As some hens scratch the bottom of their boxes it is advisable to fix an extra clump of wood upon the outside bottom. This added warmth is useful should the weather turn exceptionally cold. One breeder has had wonderful success by using a deep box covered by peat moss litter. There is also a nest

BUDGERIGAR NEST BOXES

Some of the Many Excellent Patterns From Which the Breeder May Choose

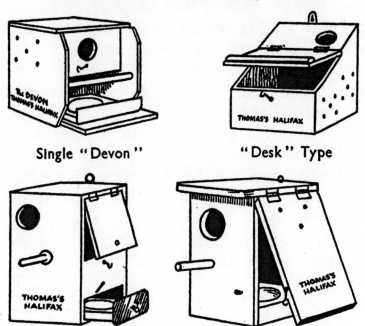

Single "Devon"   "Desk" Type

Two patterns in which the side door enables the hen to leave the nest unfrightened

Double "Devon"

[Courtesy of Messrs.
Thomas's, Halifax]

box upon the market containing two boxes in one, half of which is shut off until the hen is ready to lay her second clutch, which usually occurs before the first round leave the nest. A perch is also added for the cock bird to roost whilst an overhanging roof prevents the depredations of strange hens. A foundation of damp turf is used in this novel receptacle. This double box certainly prevents a hen seeking a new nest before her young are weaned and thus neglecting them. This box is of registered design (Reg. No. 751986-1930) and should not be imitated. In many nest boxes the bottoms are removable.

When the Birds Will Lay

Within seven days of hanging the nest boxes the pairs will commence to lay. This is provided that all birds are fit, and it must be stated here that it is fatal to pair unfit birds if strong young are needed.

Eggs are laid upon alternate days, five being the average, and incubation commences from the laying of the first egg, lasting about 17 days, the young hatching in relays.

The young require no special soft food, nature supplying the parents with a yellow fluid which is regurgitated from the crop after the manner of pigeons. This " pigeon's milk " becomes more coarse until the young are weaned. They leave the nest about a month old and soon fend for themselves. It is advisable then to remove them to a separate aviary, or they will endeavour to nest at too early an age. Six weeks with the parents should be the limit.

Nest boxes can be cleaned daily, or when necessary after the young are large enough to be moved (probably at six days old) by using a special scraper or a teaspoon. Pine sawdust helps to keep the bottoms clean, and although several writers have condemned the use of it, owing to particles entering the wind passages or ears, I have never experienced any trouble in this direction.

I have found parents most accommodating. I use several pairs for feeders of other bird's young, and exchange both eggs and young indiscriminately. For instance, I have had enormous clutches from my second rounds during the last two years. These averaged 15 eggs, although 6 is usually the limit. As some of these eggs were very valuable, I placed two under several less valuable pairs, using them as feeders, my reason for giving only two eggs each being to ensure strong babies.

It is usual for clutches of eggs, following the first round, to be laid before the young leave the nest, so that when one wants to finish the breeding season, it will be necessary to remove the nest boxes as the young leave them and to destroy any remaining eggs.

Some breeders, instead of cleaning out the nest boxes, prefer to substitute a clean nest, leaving the dirty box to be cleaned out and aired at their leisure. When so doing it is absolutely necessary to use the same type of nest box, and my experience shows that one runs a slight risk otherwise, as I have known hens refuse to enter a different box.

Other than fighting, egg-binding should be the only trouble likely to be experienced by the amateur, and this will be dealt with under the Chapter upon " Diseases ".

THE BREEDING SEASON

AS A PRELIMINARY to the commencement of breeding it is advisable to carry out a thorough inspection of breeding pens and flights. Flaws may develop in the structure, and the loss of a few good birds is to be deplored at this season. Wire netting in particular should be gone over carefully to see that it is firmly attached to the supporting standards and that it has not rusted to such an extent as to make the flight insecure. In aviaries situated near the sea, netting deteriorates fairly rapidly and it becomes brittle after two or three years although it may appear to be fairly sound. Especially should the foundations of the pens and flights be inspected for holes through which mice may gain access. If the netting used is of $\frac{1}{2}$-in. mesh, small mice will get through occasionally but $\frac{3}{8}$-in. netting will keep out any vermin.

Bottom rails of wood in pens and flights should be given a dose of wood preservative some weeks before the birds are put in and the wood tested with a knife blade for rot. Any which have become badly decayed should be replaced. If the woodwork generally has been creosoted it may require another coat, so this should be attended to as early in the year as possible, certainly not the day before the birds are being put in for breeding. Personally, I dislike creosote and prefer paint, which looks much nicer. Paint should be non-poisonous and made up with white zinc in place of white lead.

Light stone colour, in the country where the air is clean, looks well and stands weather better than most colours. Creosote is much easier to apply and probably keeps the wood even better than paint, but, after a few treatments it looks rather tarry, and the coloured wood preservatives, although nicer in appearance than creosote, are probably not much better than paint for keeping the wood and certainly do not look so well. If the aviaries are in a town where the atmosphere is smoky, creosote will probably be most suitable, but, in the open country, light paint adds greatly to the appearance of the structure.

The nest-boxes, after cleaning, should be inspected for flaws, fitted into the pens to see that they are securely suspended, and then removed once more. Perches should be examined to see that they, too, are firmly fixed, and the floors should be given a final thorough scrubbing with sand and swept clean. I know some people lime-wash the floors of pens and flights, and I think this is satisfactory. Chloride of lime will remove any green slime which may have collected on concrete flight floors; the concrete should be wet and the chloride of lime sprinkled evenly over it and left for a day or two and then thoroughly washed off.

Having attended to all these matters, having seen that all doors are secure, all bars and locks working satisfactorily, the floors of the pens should be sanded, using rather coarse sea sand, and the birds should then be installed, one pair in each pen. It is advisable, for about ten days or longer, to confine the pairs to the pens and not allow them to use the flights. If allowed to use the flights from the first birds are apt to roost out of doors at night and are more liable to be disturbed by prowling cats than if shut in until they have become accustomed to their new quarters. In these small breeding pens, where the windows are below the level of the flight roofs, it is unnecessary to have wire netting over the glass to prevent accidental escape. The space inside the pen is limited and birds cannot injure themselves by flying against the glass in this short distance. If the window is outside the flight it should be covered with wire netting, for otherwise a broken window might result in the loss of the birds, and one cannot keep little boys from throwing stones.

I mention these matters because I consider they are important; the inexperienced breeder often overlooks minor points and then complains that he has had bad luck, a flaw in his netting, a broken window, loose perches resulting in clear eggs, insecurely fixed nests resulting in accidents to the inmates, weakened springs on safety-door allowing birds to escape. Most of the bad luck is due to thoughtlessness, and although I am quite aware that one cannot foresee everything, attention to the above will help.

Having put the pairs in their respective pens, leave them alone; one must, of course, feed them night and morning, but, although it is necessary to observe, it is rarely necessary to interfere.

The birds should be watched for a few days to see that they are feeding, that the change of quarters has not made them go " soft," that all can fly strongly and that they are agreeing as prospective parents should. Hens should be watched for signs of egg-binding. Note should be kept of mating which is observed so that a check may be kept on fertility. When it is seen that the birds have settled down, that no changes require to be made, that the pairs are satisfactorily mated, the breeding-register cards should be fixed on the outside of each pen. They will have been written up with the necessary details,

Pair No., Cock No., Hen No., and the colour-capacity of each bird. For example, a pair may consist of a Cock A45/2/47, Cobalt/White and Hen A45/4/48, White Blue (deep suffusion). In the Remarks column I enter the previous breeding results of either, or both, notes regarding relationship, if any, and anything of interest during the present season such as "hen eggbound with second egg," replaced by Hen No. A45/5/48 White Blue (light suffusion). I sometimes allocate a "stick" of rings, usually five for each round, to each pair, and place these rings on a circular piece of cage wire the ends of which hook together. I also allocate a set of coloured celluloid rings for each pair, and both these sets I hang on a small hook outside the pen and adjoining the breeding-register card. Even if a few closed rings are wasted by this method, the birds in any nest being ringed in sequence is an advantage. It is better than having No. 1 a Cobalt and No. 2 a Light Yellow and No. 3 a Green, and so on. This may lead to confusion, and there is at least more chance of error. In my pens I use seed trays of large capacity, home-made affairs with three compartments so that I can give three different kinds of seed and leave the selection to the birds; I find this is less wasteful than when the seed is mixed and fed in a single dish. The trays are of wood and measure 11-in. by 4-in. by 1-in. deep, the tray being divided into two equal compartments, one of which is again subdivided into two equal spaces.

Protected against Rot.

We thus have a tray with compartments one half capacity and two compartments each one quarter. In the large compartment is put the usual stock seed, e.g., canary and millet, and in the others pin-head oats in one and in the other small one sprouted oats or greenfood. These wooden trays are finished by coating them with shellac varnish, which is harmless to the birds and which prevents moisture from rotting the wood. The trays are also easily cleaned if varnished, and can be washed out now and again and recoated. The varnish dries in a few minutes in a warm atmosphere.

I use glass pots for water and renew this daily; I have provision for automatic drinkers which flush and refill themselves, but the arrangement requires a good deal of attention and is not entirely fool-proof. With a good-sized kettle and a bucket one can wash and refill the drinkers in a few minutes, and the exercise is good for one.

About 7.30 a.m. I go round the pens and see that the birds are in good condition; that is my first concern. I next remove all the seed trays, blow off the husks and replenish them and wash and refill the drinkers. Any

I*

greenfood which is available is given at this time, and it is necessary to see that this is not frosted; it is best gathered the day before and kept in the kitchen with the roots in water overnight. If the greenfood is not given in trays, as suggested, it can be placed in glass or earthenware pots or placed in small wire holders which can be bought very cheaply and which hook on to the wire netting or wall of the pen; they are called salad racks.

Having fed the birds, I sweep up the inevitable mess of husks and, finally, inspect nests and ring the young. About an hour before dusk I again go round the seed dishes, remove any greenfood left, blow off husks and replenish the trays, this time leaving the mess until the next morning visit. It is unnecessary to poke in the nests again, and, in fact, it is inadvisable to disturb a sitting hen in the evening, as she may fail to return to the nest if put off towards nightfall. Do not put off this evening visit until it is almost dark. Birds are easily frightened then and may injure themselves. If the aviary windows face a main street it is advisable to have "black-out" frames to cover the windows. Motor-car headlights flashing through unprotected windows may upset the birds, and even put the hens off their eggs. I do not allow my breeding birds to roost out at night, but if allowed to do so the flights should be double wired.

After the breeding pairs have been in the pens for ten to fourteen days, I open the communicating doors in the mornings and allow the birds to have the use of the flights during the daytime. These doors are opened after the general clean up in the morning and are closed on the evening visit before the seed trays are filled.

This, in general, comprises the management during the breeding season. There is, of course, the ringing of young, cleaning of nests and a few other relatively unimportant matters to attend to; it must not be forgotten that budgerigars, if given a suitable nest-box and suitable food, will hatch and rear healthy young without any assistance from the owner. Where breeding is begun in February, or even earlier, egg-binding must be guarded against. The addition of cod liver oil to the seed ration is, in my opinion, a reliable preventive, and I have had none of this trouble since I have used the oil-treated seed. I regard egg-binding as being due to a vitamin deficiency, and this will be dealt with in the chapter on diseases and ailments.

Finally, I keep a small book in a pocket of the old jacket which I wear in the aviary; in this little book I jot down any interesting facts and observations; it is a great aid, and I recommend the practice to all breeders.

MANAGEMENT IN THE BREEDING SEASON

I AM one of those who does not believe in commencing the breeding season very early. The last week in February or the first week in March is soon enough for me. Some breeders begin operations as soon as the New Year arrives, and in isolated cases we hear of chicks in the nest boxes at Christmas ! I suppose that one reason for making such an unseasonable commencement is the alluring prospect of having very advanced youngsters for the Breeders' Classes at the earlier shows. But, frankly, I do not think the game is worth the candle. I have seen some disastrous results in establishments where breeding has commenced in January.

I think the majority of fanciers make a beginning in March, which provides sufficient time for the second round youngsters to complete their baby moult before the nights are long and the sunshine and warmth of summer are no more.

If the last clutches are not hatched until late August or early September the chicks miss in the earliest days of their lives—when their future health can be made or marred—those advantages which are enjoyed by the older youngsters, the sunshine, the longer hours of daylight and their genial warmth, the wild greens and the seeding grasses.

Chicks which have their first moult in late autumn or in the winter usually change their feathers slowly, and a slow moult is never as satisfactory as a normal one.

Youngsters born in the fall of the year are often slow in their development and it is not advisable to breed from them in the following season.

All this provides an argument against those who are opposed to making a commencement before April, and those who even advocate deferring putting the nest boxes up until May is in.

But of much greater importance than the date when the fancier commences the season is the condition of the birds when they are mated. It is of vital importance that they should be ripe for breeding before they are provided with nest boxes. If this rule is strictly observed, the possibilities of egg binding, infertility, and eggs being cast out of the boxes by the hen, are reduced to a minimum.

Budgerigars are only in the desired state to go to nest when they are in perfect health, alert and full of life and activity, free from any sign of moult, with their feathers tight fitting and carrying that bloom which denotes physical fitness, with their wattles bright in colour, and when they are displaying obvious signs of desire to breed.

If you follow my advice you will have prepared all your matings on paper some time before you even think of actually putting the pairs together. As the cock and the hen in each of the pairs on the list both come into the condition which I have described, then and then only should they go into their breeding quarters. Obviously the pairs will not be ready simultaneously and, therefore, it is unusual for one to be able to mate all the pairs on a specially selected day. The actual mating process is generally spread over a period.

Breeding Ages

There are differences of opinion as to the minimum ages at which cocks and hens respectively should be mated, but I think it can be accepted that the average view of the breeders as a whole is that cocks should not breed until they are ten months old and hens not until they are eleven months old, though in our own aviaries we do not lay down quite such a hard and fast rule. We allow the actual development of the individual to govern the matter to a certain extent. Some birds seem to mature more rapidly than others, and one can exercise a little licence in such cases. All the same, the figures I give above are safe ones, and I advise my readers to adhere to them approximately, bearing in mind that as a general rule it is preferable for the birds to be older rather than younger than the minimum ages stated, if the fancier can so arrange matters.

Some authorities fix the minimum breeding age for cocks at eleven months and that for hens at twelve months ; and there are, to my knowledge, a few fanciers who do not mate their hens until the second year after their birth. Personally I do not consider there to be any wisdom in suppressing a hen's natural instincts for so long after she has attained her full sexual development.

As to the maximum age at which Budgerigars can be employed satisfactorily for the breeding of high-class stock, this is to a great extent dependent on the vigour and condition of the individual. Some specimens are still hale and hearty at an age when others have become almost decrepit. Cocks can be used for more years than can hens, because the propagation of the species is not so demanding of the male as it is of the female.

When I am asked to express the maximum safe breeding age for cocks and hens respectively my answer is six years for cocks and four years for hens, but, as I have indicated above, these figures are subject to variation governed by the state of particular individuals, and I have had reported to me quite satisfactory results from cocks older than six and hens as old as six.

Youth and Age

I do not advise ever mating two quite old Budgerigars together. They should each be provided with mates younger than themselves.

Before the pairs are put into their breeding quarters they should be ringed with open, coloured celluloid rings. On each bird of a pair you place a ring of the same colour, on the opposite leg to that carrying the metal rings, of course. Before the youngsters from that pair are taken away from their parents you put on to their legs celluloid rings again of the same colour. Thus if the adults are ringed with blue rings, all their progeny of that season will also wear blue rings. This is a great advantage when later young birds of different breeding are flying together in an aviary, because one can tell at a glance without catching it just how any particular youngster is bred.

Under every occupied nest box there should be pinned a card bearing the following wording, and with ample space provided for entering the various particulars indicated by the headings which I have had printed in capital letters :—

AVIARY No. 2.   COLOURED RING : Red.
PAIR No. 6.
COCK : Dark Green/blue, W50/34/50.
HEN : Cobalt, W50/117/49.
FIRST EGG LAID : March 7th.
DUE TO HATCH : March 27th.
NO. OF EGGS : 6.
NO. OF YOUNGSTERS : 5.
RING NOS. : 42.
        43.
        44.
        45.
        46.   Transferred to pair No. 7.
REMARKS : Hen broke one egg.

These Breeding Cards should be used in conjunction with *Cage Birds* Budgerigar Breeding and Show Register, which I describe fully in Chapter XX. The Breeding Cards are for rough notes, the Breeding Register for a more permanent record. The Breeding Register can be utilised alone, without the cards if the owner so desires—and this will certainly save his time—but the Breeding

Cards cannot be satisfactorily employed without the Breeding Register. The latter provides for the recording of the following essential information :—

Pair No. ; Cock ; Hen; Theoretical expectation (that is the colours of the youngsters which the pair can produce; Date mated ; In Aviary No. ; Coloured Ring ; Date first egg laid ; Due to hatch ; No. of eggs ; No. of chicks ; Ring numbers ; Colour ; Sex ; Remarks.

As in the Register there are spaces for the recording of all the particulars set forth on a Breeding Card, in addition to other important particulars, it will be understood that the only advantage of using the Cards as an auxiliary to the Register is that they tell at a glance as the owner goes round the breeding compartments the progress of each pair of birds. Many breeders, I believe, use the Register without the Cards, merely pinning under each occupied nest box a card bearing the number of the pair in occupation.

Also of importance during the breeding season are those other sections of *Cage Birds* Breeding and Show Register which I have dealt with in Chapter XX, viz : *Descriptions of Parent Birds* and the *Young Bird Register*.

Where more than one pair of Budgerigars are to occupy the same house, each pair should be kept in a show cage for a week or more prior to their being allowed into the aviary. The object of this preliminary caging is to induce the cocks and hens constituting the respective pairs to become so attached to each other that they will keep to their own mates when they are in their breeding quarters.

But even when " courtship " has been conducted in the manner I have described, there is no guarantee that mate changing will not occur. The fewer pairs there are in one place, the less the risk of the pedigrees of the youngsters not being as the owner wishes them to be ; but even when there are only two pairs it is not uncommon for the two cocks to change wives. And where more than one pair are housed together, so unfaithful are Budgerigar cocks on occasions, that one bird may actually be the sire of all the youngsters in the different nests ! All this is, of course, the strongest possible evidence in support of the one-pair breeding system as compared with colony breeding.

Fighting Females

But there is another danger in keeping more than one pair together which is even more serious than that of cocks which are not faithful to the hens which we have selected for them. I refer to fighting hens.

Hens are at any time more pugnacious than cocks, although when kept together in the winter, separated from the cocks, fights seldom occur; but when they are breeding their pugnacity is increased fourfold. Compared with hens at this season cocks are docility personified. If two hens select the same nest box, both determined to retain it, a fine old brawl will there be between them. If one hen is sitting on eggs or nursing chicks, and another hen enters the nest box, whether by accident or design, there will be a fight to the death, all the eggs or chicks being destroyed too, unless the owner discovers what is transpiring and separates the belligerents before serious damage is done.

I have known a hen to be so bellicose when mated that to allow her to breed in the same place as another pair was simply to court the death of the other hen. Without any cause whatever a hen of this disposition will attack another hen savagely, with often a fatal result.

The Best Safeguard

I do not want it to be inferred from what I have written about fighting hens that battles in the aviaries are usual or frequent. They are not. In most cases all goes well, the birds live together in harmony, and each pair rears good clutches of chicks without let or hindrance. Nevertheless, the danger of the homicidal hen is one which must be guarded against, and the best preventative is the one-pair-per-place system, which also ensures perfect control of pedigrees, so essential where the breeder is establishing a strain on the lines described in Chapter XI.

If circumstances make the keeping of more than one pair in one aviary unavoidable, then the best protection against fighting hens is the provision of plenty of nest boxes, at least two to each pair. These should all be of one pattern and colour, and all hung well up on the walls of the shelter or house part of the aviary and all at the same height. When only one pair occupy a place, only one nest box is necessary.

It is very many years since I discontinued the erstwhile universal practice of keeping several breeding pairs together—known as the colony system. Practically no breeder of exhibition Budgerigars now follows any other method than that of keeping one pair in one aviary or cage, thus ensuring complete control of his pedigrees and perfect protection against pugnacity.

In times past great were the arguments for and against cage breeding. Experience has taught me that cage breeding is superior to colony breeding, to which in many establishments it is the sole or partial alternative. Cage breeding can be conducted with complete success providing the cages are all they ought to be, and are in a suitable room, correct in every particular as regards light, ventilation and general construction. It is, however, imperative that the adults should not be kept in the cages a week longer than is necessary and that the chicks are transferred to aviaries as soon as they leave their parents. At Lintonholme we breed in both single-pair aviaries and cages.

When the single-pair system (sometimes termed control breeding) is employed, it is not necessary to put the pair in a show cage for a preparatory courtship. They can go straight into cage or aviary. But it is not advisable to hang up the nest box for four or five days. This gives the birds time in which to settle down, and avoids the rather abnormal sexual excitement which the appearance of a mate and a nest box simultaneously sometimes engenders, with often undesirable results, such as the throwing out of eggs as they are laid.

The First Egg

As soon as the hen—and often the cock as well—is regularly going in and out of the nest box, it will not be long before the first egg is laid. I am not able to say how many days it will be after the nest boxes are put up before the hen will lay, as they vary in this respect according to their condition, but ten days is about the average length of time. It is not necessary to put anything in the box in the form of nest material. The hen will lay on the bare wood, though she and her mate frequently make a few small wood shavings by gnawing, and which you will see in the basin of the nest box. These shavings serve no good purpose. No doubt the birds when making them are obeying an old instinct of the wild Budgerigars, which had to make or improve their nests by boring into the trees.

The hen lays on alternate days until she has completed the clutch, which may consist of any number of eggs up to nine, though larger clutches have often been recorded. But even a nest of nine is above the normal, and an average of five may be considered to be perfectly satisfactory. If I secure an average of four in the first round and five in the second I am very well satisfied. In fact, an average of six per pair is sufficient to cause one to be quite pleased. Hens usually have larger second clutches than first clutches, particularly maiden hens.

The period of incubation is eighteen days. The hen does not always commence sitting with the laying of the first egg. Sometimes she waits until the second egg is laid. Therefore, I always calculate the date of hatching at twenty days from the appearance of the first egg.

The hen does all the sitting, and the cock feeds her. She feeds the chicks in the box. The cock helps her, if she will allow him to do so, which is by no means always the case. Both feed the chicks for a time after they have left the nest.

The method of feeding is that of regurgitation, which means the pumping into the crops of the babies food which has been eaten by the parents, mixed with the gastric juices, and made to just that right consistency for the youngsters' digestive organs to deal with it efficiently and for them to obtain the maximum amount of nutrition from it.

Sequence of Hatching

As the eggs are laid on alternate days, it naturally follows that the chicks hatch on varying dates, and in a clutch of five, for example, we can have one youngster ten days old when the last chick has only just hatched, and there is a marked difference in the sizes of the babies. This is not really desirable, even though with the Budgerigar it is perfectly natural. It cannot be disputed that when in a nest containing chicks of uneven sizes one dies, it is usually the smallest and therefore the weakest and the most likely to suffer if there is any lack of attention on the part of the parents.

To overcome this objection to the Budgerigar's natural system of laying its eggs on alternate days, and the chicks, therefore, varying in age and size, some fanciers have tried the experiment of lifting the first one, two, or three eggs that are laid, placing them carefully in suitable boxes in sawdust, replacing them with pot eggs, and only allowing the hen to commence incubating her eggs after, say, the laying of her third egg. This system is that adopted regularly by Canary breeders, and, apparently, with complete success. This practice is not followed with my wife's birds, and I do not advise it. Obviously in the case of an establishment of some size, the extra work entailed by conducting this procedure will be of no small moment.

Those who have sent me reports on their experiments in this direction have told me that they have not found it safe to lift more than two eggs. In many instances where they have extended the procedure to three eggs the first egg to be removed has failed to hatch.

"Distributing" the Chicks

My own method of equalising the sizes of the chicks as much as possible is by changing them about from nest to nest, putting large ones with large ones and small ones with small ones. In the same way, it being inadvisable to allow a pair to rear more than four chicks at one time, or at the most five—and then only when unavoidable—if we have, say, three in one nest and five in another we give the pair with three one youngster from the nest of five, leaving them with four each. By the exercise of a little thought changes can usually be made without difficulty which will leave the position of all the clutches in the establishment as we desire it.

Fortunately, Budgerigars are most accommodating in this direction. They do not object to the appearance of a few strange babies in the nest box, and if they have an eye for dimensions and if they do discover that some of the children are not their own, so strong is their parental instinct that they simply don't care, and carry on blithely as though the family was all their own !

There are recorded cases when a cock has died at the time when there were youngsters in the nest box, of a new cock being introduced and of his having carried on as step-father without hesitation and with complete success. At Lintonholme we have done this on two occasions. Once it was quite successful, but in the other case, the youngsters were killed. We shall not do it again !

Records Essential

In changing chicks about from nest to nest either for the purpose of equalising sizes, equalising numbers, or because, as sometimes occurs, the adults are proving to be bad feeders, the owner must keep a complete record of all the transfers so that he does not lose trace of the actual parents of the youngsters moved—in other words does not run the risk of being unable to record their pedigrees accurately.

This danger can be completely avoided by ringing the chicks before they are changed, leaving the ring numbers on the Breeding Card of the real parents, but writing thereon " Transferred to Pair No. —." An accurate account of all transfers must be kept in this way.

I have found that occasionally there arises the necessity to transfer a little baby when it is really too small to ring. In this case in order to ensure that the record of its parentage shall not be lost, it has to be placed under a pair which are of such a colour that the colour of the transferred chick when it is fledging will indicate that it is the stranger. For example, you can change a youngster from a pair of Light Greens to a pair of Light Yellows without any fear of losing track of it. The appearance of a Light Green in a nest consisting of Light Yellows will tell you all you want to know.

When the hen is sitting on eggs I think it is advisable to disturb her as little as possible except for an occasional glance in the nest box prior to her having completed her laying to ensure that she is not suffering from egg-binding, a trouble which I shall refer to more fully later in this chapter.

After hatching I believe in looking inside the boxes every other day or, still better, every day. Most hens soon become accustomed to the owner inspecting their babies, and I do not see how these periodical examinations can do any harm. On the other hand, they can be a definite advantage.

For one thing they lead to the discovery of any chick which may have died, and which if it were not removed would decompose and emit an offensive smell which would be injurious to the other youngsters.

In Chapter VI I referred to those particularly dirty nests which sometimes occur with frequency when certain birds are occupying them. These would not receive the attention which they should have if regular inspections of the nests were not conducted.

And then a box containing young birds has to be opened in any case whenever one or more is at the age for ringing.

How to Fit Rings

The closed metal ring authorised by the Budgerigar Society can be slipped on to the chicks' legs without the slightest pain, in less than a minute, at approximately four or five days after hatching. The method of ringing is as follows :—

Take the bird from the nest box, place the ring over the two front toes and pass over the ball of the foot ; then with a match, pointed by burning, insert under the small toe and pull through. In the same way the other toe is passed through the ring.

Another way is to pass the three long toes through the ring, then slip the ring over the ball of the foot, and pull through the remaining toe with a match pointed by burning.

The rings are ordered from the Ring Secretary of the Budgerigar Society and supplied by officially appointed ring makers. The marks on each ring consist of a code number, serial number, and the numbers indicating the year of issue, e.g. H11–121–48. H11 is the code number, 121 the serial number, and 48 the year number.

Every member of the Budgerigar Society and the Area Budgerigar Societies is allotted a code number and this gives him or her the right to have it stamped on all rings purchased. Thus the name of the breeder of every bird so ringed can be instantly traced by reference to the Societies' Year Books in which there is published annually a list of the members' names and addresses and code numbers. It is usual for a member to instruct the ring maker to commence the serial numbering of his or her rings at 1 every year, though this is not imperative.

Dirty Nest Boxes

I have referred above to those particularly dirty nest boxes which occur with some pairs of Budgerigars. These birds are what we know as " dirty feeders." They distribute seed all over the inside of the boxes, it becomes mixed with excreta, and a fine old mess there is visible to the owner when he is on his tour of inspection.

The nest box can be easily cleaned, of course, but a worse evil of these dirty feeders is that they plaster the chicks' faces at each feeding with almost as much regurgitated food as they pump into their crops.

This, often mixed with a quantity of excreta, sets into a cement-like substance, which, unless it is removed *very frequently*, has a most damaging effect on the beaks of the youngsters. It definitely retards the growth of the upper mandible, which at that tender age is weak and sensitive. The lower mandible, being stronger, continues its normal development, outgrows the upper mandible, and the result is what is known as an undershot beak, which is very unsightly and a blemish which makes a bird absolutely useless for exhibition.

The owner should clean the beaks of the chicks whenever he discovers the cement-like substance adhering to their faces.

Inheritance of Undershot Beaks

Sometimes, due to the same cause, the beak does not actually become undershot, but the upper mandible develops a thin and corrugated appearance, and in some cases the tip of the beak is distorted. These beaks may come right in time, but often they never acquire their natural strength and shape.

Some authorities contend that undershot beaks can also be inherited. I have never been able to convince myself of the accuracy of this statement, although I admit that I have no proof that *some* undershot beaks are not due to the cause I have above described but are an inherited characteristic. And it may be that some undershot beaks are attributable to a rickety condition.

Certain it is that theoretically there is no reason why parents or brothers and sisters of youngsters which have undershot beaks definitely known to be attributable to "dirty feeding" should not be used for breeding purposes. In fact, the bird itself with the undershot beak caused in this way will not necessarily breed chicks with undershot beaks, because it is a proven genetic truth that *acquired* characteristics are not handed down. Nevertheless, I have always taken the absolutely safe course—and I advise my readers to do likewise—of not breeding from or selling a bird which has, or ever had, a malformed beak. It is true that undershot mouths are inherited in dogs, and in some cases in Budgerigars they may be due to inheritance. I still have an open mind on the subject.

A dirty nest box is also a positive danger to the feet of the chicks. They become clotted with the cement-like substance to which I have referred, it sets hard, and can have most damaging effects. If the attachment is discovered before it becomes solid it can be detached without much difficulty with the fingers. Later the toes have to be carefully soaked in warm water and the adhering material removed. If this is attempted without soaking, there is a grave risk of one or more toe nails being torn away. When the adults are fed on the right kinds of seed, dirty nests do not often occur, which is fortunate. Some fanciers practically never experience them.

Egg-Binding

Some people look incredulous when I tell them, quite truthfully, that I have never personally experienced a case of egg-binding in Budgerigars—in other words, the inability of the hen to dispel the egg at the moment when normally it should be laid—yet it is a danger for which the breeder must ever be observant. If a hen is egg-bound and immediate and successful action is not taken, she will surely die. Maiden hens laying their first egg are probably the most likely subject for eggs binding, although cases often occur with unfit or very old hens—and it is not always the first egg of a clutch which becomes bound.

As soon as a case of egg-binding is discovered, the hen should be placed in a cage and put before a hot fire, olive oil being applied to the vent by a feather.

If these measures fail, there is a more drastic treatment, but I do not advise it except as a last resource, and after heat and olive oil have been given every opportunity of succeeding. It is the pigeon fanciers' method and consists of putting a piece of muslin over a small basin containing boiling water. You hold the suffering hen over the muslin, the steam ascends from the boiling water, and, if all goes well, the egg is dropped on to the muslin. She must not be suspended over the steam for more than a few seconds at a time.

Egg-binding is often due to the hen not really being in good breeding condition. A general opinion is that a course of cod liver oil feeding, as described in Chapter VII, up to the time when the hen lays her first egg is a most effective preventative.

Neglected Chicks

Although Budgerigars are as a rule exceedingly good parents, just as they are comparatively prolific breeders, occasionally a pair of birds neglect their chicks either by ceasing to feed them or only half feeding them. Non-feeding means a quick death; half feeding means retarded growth and a badly grown youngster, which will never mature into a vigorous, healthy adult. Therefore, it is clear that as soon as the discovery is made that the parents are not giving proper attention to their offspring, the chicks must be removed to another pair, consisting, if possible, of birds which the owner knows he can rely on to do their work as it should be done.

Although I am referring here to those troubles which infrequently occur when young Budgerigars are in the nest box, I do not want any of my readers to get the impression that normally they have many of these difficulties to contend with, because such is not the case. In fact, Budgerigar fanciers have but few worries compared with breeders of many other kinds of livestock. Nevertheless, we have to tackle problems as they arise in a cheerful, philosophic way, and with the determination to overcome them. It is well, therefore, that I should describe the most common obstacles which have to be combated on occasions, so that the novices who read this book may be prepared for them.

Infantile Mortality

Great breeders and rearers as Budgerigars are, the beginner must not expect *too* much. In any season there is no such thing as a large number of eggs in every nest, 100 per cent. fertility, 100 per cent. hatching, and 100 per cent. rearing. For instance, we all lose some chicks, particularly when they are very young, without any apparent cause.

There are (say) five young ones in a box, all as far as can be seen equally strong. One morning we find that two are dead, yet the others go on and prosper. Why did those two die? If I could dogmatically reply to that question I should have solved a riddle which has perplexed me all my life. Sometimes we can supply the answer. Frequently we cannot do so. The problem of mortality in young birds and animals is a formidable one, and the greatest authorities have not been able to discover a complete solution.

Budgerigar breeders have the satisfaction of knowing that with these birds the infantile mortality percentage is low compared with the percentage in some other species of livestock, and so long as the deaths of chicks do not become abnormal, they can rest content and realise that most of their contemporaries are faring no better, many of them probably worse.

It is when deaths are numerous that a serious review of the situation has to be made. Steps must then be taken to discover, if possible, what is wrong with housing, feeding, management, or the parent birds, to cause the excessive mortality.

Usually when chicks die through not being fed, this apparent neglect on the part of the parents can be explained by the fact that the babies are too weak to " ask " for food in the natural way. Then the old birds do not bother about them.

Normally in Budgerigar keeping everything runs along smoothly, but it is surprising how breeding seasons vary. One year nothing goes wrong, the next year unexpected difficulties arise and the result of our efforts fails to satisfy. We all have our good cycles and our bad cycles, in spite of there being no change in our management or feeding or the condition of the parent birds, which makes us agree with Shakespeare that there are more things in Heaven and Earth than are dreamt of in our philosophy.

Be of Good Cheer

It is the fancier who accepts reverses with equanimity and a determination to overcome all obstacles who ultimately achieves his or her ambitions as a breeder. We must ever use our failures as the teachers of lessons which will serve us well in the future, benefit by our errors, and turn our misfortunes into blessings in disguise.

I am digressing, but I desire to cheer those novices who may be discouraged by any of those untoward occurrences which I describe in this chapter.

Now to return to more practical matters. I have on rare, very rare occasions known Budgerigar cocks die through an excess of zeal in feeding the hen and chicks. They have literally fed themselves to death, feeding away each evening all the food in their crops and going to their perches for the night without retaining any seed for their own nutrition.

When we catch a cock pining in this way we take him away from the hen until he has had time to have a few good meals and recuperate from his deprivation. The hen attends to the wants of the family in the meantime. After the cock has been replaced in the aviary we keep a watchful eye on him to see that he is not repeating behaviour which but for our timely intervention would probably have caused his death. A cock which is starving himself in this manner loses his tightness of feather and his alertness and has a mopy appearance.

That defective feathering which is described as French Moult can usually be detected before the youngsters leave the nest box, though sometimes it is not until the chicks are out in the aviary that this displeasing condition asserts itself. As I propose dealing with this disease at some length in Chapter XXII, nothing more will be said about it here, and I will pass on to another annoyance which occasionally occurs, viz., that of feather plucking.

This practice on the part of one parent—I think it is usually the hen—consists of the deliberate plucking or biting off of the feathers as soon as the babies begin to fledge. Sometimes the feathers are pulled right out, but from my observation it is more usual for them to be nipped off close to the skin.

The best thing to do when a pair start feather plucking is to remove the youngsters to another pair, if possible. If this cannot be done, then put the chicks into another nest box close to the original box. Make sure that the cock finds them, which as a rule he soon will do. Then the hen will confine her attention to the old box, in which she will lay her next clutch of eggs, the cock will attend to the babies in the adjoining box and they may well be saved from further plucking.

In some cases after the first moult of a feather-plucked youngster the feathers grow naturally on the bare parts, but this is not by any means always the case ; in fact, I think that in most instances these birds are never quite normally feathered. At least, I have noticed for over twelve months after the date of hatching a deficiency in both the length and the quality of the feathers which have grown on plucked areas.

As to whether the tendency to feather plucking is inheritable or not, I am not yet prepared to say, but it is a possibility which must not be overlooked. If it is proved that feather-pluckers can transmit this unfortunate nervous practice to their offspring, then birds bred from them must neither be bred from nor sold ; and, of course, it is unwise in any case to allow a feather-plucker to rear any more youngsters when once the pre-disposition has been dis-covered, because a repetition of the offence is almost a certainty. Some fanciers, when they find that a clutch of chicks are being plucked, and they are unable to transfer them to foster parents, smear them with some offensive-smelling oil. (Cod liver oil is sometimes recommended for this purpose.) This is a messy business, and I do not advise it, unless absolutely unavoidable.

There is an old theory that in excessively hot and dry summers lack of humidity in the atmosphere is calculated to cause chicks to die before hatching, due to the membranes in the egg becoming so tough that the chick cannot break through them to chip the shell. It is to counteract this condition that moisture is artificially provided by poultry fanciers when eggs are being incubated, the object being to prevent excessive evaporation of the natural moisture in the egg.

Lack of humidity on very hot days can to a certain extent be counteracted by spraying the walls and floors of the aviaries with cold water. At Lintonholme we neither provide moisture in the nests nor spray water about the houses.

Although as I have indicated " dead in shell " may be attributable to dryness of the atmosphere, I do not think it is so frequently responsible as it is usually alleged to be. The natural weakness of some chicks is, in my opinion, more often than not the reason for their inability to hatch, and in such cases it is better that they should die rather than be born and be for ever weaklings.

Personally, I have not found " dead in shell " to be so common with Budgerigars as it is with some breeds of pigeons, and I am convinced that providing the parent birds are virile, the greater mortality is after the chicks have hatched and when they are very young. At least that has always been my experience.

The embryo sometimes succumbs to its own natural weakness before it has materialised beyond the embryonic stage, and then the egg is what is termed " addled." But addled eggs can be due to neglectful sitting by the hen during the period of incubation. She may leave the nest for so lengthy a time that the eggs become cold before she returns—a very rare occurrence—or, of course, she may desert them altogether.

Red Mite

Red mite is the most difficult of all parasites to eradicate completely from an aviary, and it is the only one which causes any serious trouble to Budgerigar fanciers; in fact, no other pest need be feared if aviaries and all appliances are kept scrupulously clean.

Red mite will make their presence felt at times even in the cleanest establishment. They dwell in cracks and crevices in the woodwork. They are not to be seen by day but they come out in myriads at night, suck the blood of the birds, and change in colour from grey to red. By daylight they have disappeared, only to commence their marauding again when darkness arrives.

Paraffin brushed in freely in all the likely places for red mite to inhabit is a useful preventative. So is creosote, but unfortunately some time after it has dried it seems to lose its offensiveness to the mite, which blithely ignore it; and it is not advisable in any case to have creosote that is not absolutely dry where the birds can reach it. Some of the strong proprietary disinfectants can also be recommended, and their odour is less unpleasant to birds and owners than paraffin. These are frequently advertised in *Cage Birds*.

As far as nest boxes are concerned, immersion in boiling water is the best procedure, and always before nest boxes used in a previous season are again placed in the aviaries they should be thoroughly scrubbed and then soaked again in boiling water. The use of cardboard nest boxes as described in Chapter VIII obviates this task. Every precaution should be taken by the adoption of such means as I have described to prevent a serious invasion of these parasites because they can adversely affect the health of Budgerigars, their constant blood-sucking conducing to a debilitated condition; and it is now contended that they are the cause of French Moult—a theory about which I will have more to say in Chapter XXII.

Occasionally the owner may find in the nest box a chick blown up with wind until it is like a small balloon, and it usually dies. The common idea is that this is a symptom of indigestion and probably that is what it is on most occasions.

Many years ago my aviary attendant, after close observation of a number of youngsters afflicted in the manner described found that the nostrils of these babies were completely closed up either with dirt or with dry, cemented food, and that because of there being no passage through the nostrils it was impossible for the birds to exhale. Consequently wind gathered in the crops of the chicks when they were being fed by their parents, resulting in the balloon-like appearance above referred to.

I have not found evidence to make me disagree with this contention, and here we have another reason why fanciers should keep the chicks' faces clean.

Some breeders put sawdust or husks in the basin of the nest box instead of leaving the wood bare. Although I have not yet convinced myself that there is any material advantage in doing this, there is no disadvantage, unless it be the risk of sawdust getting into the mouths of newly-hatched chicks, and which causes me to prefer husks to sawdust, though in our own aviaries we use neither.

I have advisedly warned the novices who read this book of the difficulties with which they will have to contend at times, yet I again emphasise the fact that the majority of young Budgerigars flourish exceedingly from the moment they are hatched, and when they are 30 days old, or thereabouts, they leave the boxes and fly into the aviary—beautiful little creatures—clean, tight feathered, lively, and a delightful sight for any bird lover to behold.

The parents continue to feed them for a week or more, but very soon they commence to pick, and are able within a few days to consume sufficient food daily fully to satisfy their appetites. But the adults do not then cease to feed the babies, and I consider it advisable to leave them with the old birds for eight to ten days, that is until they are about 40 days old. No first-round youngsters must be left with their parents after the second-round chicks have commenced to hatch, and I do not like to see chicks still with their father and mother when the eggs of the second clutch are being incubated. Particularly when the birds are breeding in cages do some young ones develop the habit of going back into the box, to the discomfiture of the sitting hen.

I advise that seed for the youngsters should be placed in pots or trays, perchance at first they experience any difficulty in finding their way to the hoppers.

Before transferring young ones to the " nursery " I keep them for a fortnight in the bird room in the training cages (which are occupied in the winter by the birds which are being prepared for exhibition, and which I will describe in Chapter XVII), running with them for the first days at least one or two adults to lead them to the food, grit, and water vessels.

This early training gives to the youngsters a steadiness which does not desert them for the remainder of their lives, and which makes it all the easier later to train them to comport themselves gracefully in the show cages when they are being prepared for competition at the shows.

" Nursery Days "

From these training cages the young birds are transferred to the " nurseries," which are reasonably large aviaries, in which they can secure an abundance of fresh air and exercise, which assists their development enormously. Again I provide open feeding receptacles instead of hoppers and again I introduce a few old birds to guide them to their food. After three or four days these adults can be removed if the owner so desires.

I have previously indicated the evils of overcrowding, which is never more undesirable than when the young stock is in a " nursery."

A careful daily inspection should be made to see that all the youngsters are progressing satisfactorily. If any appear weakly they should be removed ; otherwise their more vigorous fellows may " chivy " them off the food and generally make their lives unpleasant.

And this reminds me of an important instruction to which I must give expression, viz : all " bad doers " either in the nest box or " nursery " must be carefully recorded in the Breeding Register, because these birds must never be bred from—however satisfactory they may be in appearance later—for all those good reasons on which I have expounded at length in Chapters XI and XIII.

Two Families Only

In several places in this book I stress the golden rule of not taking more than two nests per season from each pair. The temptation to rear the extra clutch of chicks can be great, but it should be resisted with determination.

The third nest is asking too much of the physical capacity of the adults. It takes so much out of them that it makes them unreliable for breeding purposes in the following season, and if they are exhibition specimens, the strain which the third nest involves makes it more difficult to get them into show condition.

Further, third-round chicks are almost invariably less vigorous than their older brothers and sisters, and, therefore, themselves less suitable as parents when they in turn attain the age for breeding. These birds sold to other fanciers will probably fail to give satisfaction, and the spread of such specimens throughout the aviaries of this country can actually damage the whole race of domesticated Budgerigars, just as can similar injury be done by the sale to unsuspecting purchasers of birds which have been " bad doers " as babies or which have suffered from illness and have merely been " patched up."

Now the implementing of the " two nests only " rule calls for further explanation. Its real implication is that a pair of Budgies should only be allowed to *feed* two nests. It is the feeding which taxes the systems of the parents and not so much, in the case of the hen, the laying and the sitting. Therefore, if you find that every egg of a clutch is infertile, or if all the eggs are addled or the chicks " dead in shell," or if for any other reason no young are forthcoming, you need not count that as one round. In due course the parents will throw out the eggs and prepare to go to nest again, which you can let them do.

The fact that it is the feeding which puts the most strain on the adults gives the clue to the reason why so many exhibitors make a practice of holding over a number of young cocks—some also apply the system to hens—without breeding from them in the season following the year of their birth. This is a particularly desirable procedure in the case of second-round youngsters.

The birds selected for the purpose are usually those which show the most promise of developing into good exhibition specimens. Undoubtedly by not having to feed youngsters in the first full year of their lives they mature more rapidly and are the more likely to be successful show birds earlier in their careers than otherwise would be the case.

Of course, it is almost a practical impossibility for an owner to keep unmated all his promising young cocks for an entire season, but modifications of the principle can be applied to some yearlings from which one actually does obtain chicks in the first season.

For instance, from some, particularly those hatched in, say, late June or early July, one nest only may be taken in the following summer.

Sometimes I allow a young cock which has the appearance of being a prize winner to fertilise the eggs but not to feed the chicks. This is avoided by transferring the eggs to another pair of birds, if, of course, there is a pair available ; or they can be divided between two pairs.

Foster-Parent or " Feeders "

In order to ensure always having birds so situated that the fancier is able to place in their nests eggs lifted for the reasons above described, or chicks which are being unsatisfactorily tended by their own parents, or chicks which have to be transferred to avoid pairs having to feed too many youngsters and thus break " the not more than four or five " rule, the most efficient method is to use birds kept specially for the purpose of serving as foster-parents or "feeders." This system is operated extensively by pigeon fanciers, and I know of no reason why it should not be of equal assistance to Budgerigar breeders.

A number of pairs of Budgerigars, which must be strong and healthy but which can be inexpensive and of no merit when judged by exhibition standards, is all that is required. The actual quantity of these " feeders " to be mated simultaneously with the mating of the pedigree stock will be governed by the number of pairs of the latter and, of course, by the accommodation at the owner's disposal. In fact, the only possible objection to the use of foster-parents is that the fancier whose aviaries are limited in size and number may not be able to spare the additional space to house these birds satisfactorily. The more pairs of "feeders" kept, the greater the chance that there will always be pairs ready to take charge of eggs or chicks when they are required to do so. Modified colony breeding can be practised in the case of feeders, though it is essential for them to have settled down and be living together in harmony before eggs or chicks from the pedigree stock are transferred to them. We do not use "feeders" in our own establishment now because we breed from so many pairs that we never seem to be in difficulties when it is desired to transfer chicks from one pair to another.

The feeding of the adult birds in the breeding aviaries and the youngsters in the "nursery" I have written about at length in Chapter VII and, therefore, there is no need for me to repeat my opinions here, beyond saying that feeding when Budgerigars are breeding is of paramount importance, probably more so than at any other season of the year.

I have already explained that owing to the varying condition of the birds one cannot start them all off breeding simultaneously at the commencement of the season and, therefore, it automatically follows that they will not all have completed rearing their two clutches of eggs at exactly the same time.

Novices sometimes describe to me a difficulty which they have when they want to bring breeding operations to a close, due to the fact that before the last chick of the second nest has left the box the hen has almost invariably laid again. It is the sacrificing of these eggs which is repugnant to the owner. He finds it difficult to resist the temptation to let the hen continue sitting, and almost before he realises what is happening he is allowing the pair to rear a third batch of chicks, which is entirely contrary to wise policy.

However unsentimental and sacrificial the action may appear to be, these third-round eggs should be destroyed, or put under another pair, as soon as the last chick has left the nest. Then the boxes should be taken down and the pair of birds left to feed the second-round youngsters for eight to ten days, when the cock should be separated from the hen.

In our own aviaries we often avoid the hen laying before the second clutch of chicks has left the nest by taking the cock away when the youngest chick is about a fortnight old, leaving the hen to complete the rearing of the youngsters entirely by herself. Anyone who adopts this practice must observe closely if the hen is feeding properly, and if any lack of attention is noticed the cock must be returned immediately, though rarely, if ever, will this necessity arise.

There is an additional advantage in this procedure, viz.: by taking cocks away from the hens in the manner described, more time is provided in which to prepare them for exhibition.

Colour Varieties

In some countries, particularly Belgium and France, the breeding of various coloured Budgerigars, especially the blue variety, is highly developed and of late also in Germany and Austria, many fanciers are turning to the breeding of coloured specimens. In the bird periodicals of France, Belgium and England coloured Budgerigars, mostly blue ones, are regularly offered for sale. At the great bird shows a wide range of coloured varieties are displayed.

All animals which have become domesticated and bred in captivity for many years are inclined to change their colour. In the case of birds there is, as with domestic poultry, the tendency to become white, called albinism, that is, the disappearance of any pigment from the plumage, and in the case of the canary and also of the Budgerigar, there exists the tendency to become yellow, which is only a first step towards albinism.

The absence of pigment in the plumage is a symptom of degeneration which must not be connected with degeneration of the whole organism.

But considering that all coloured Budgerigars, no matter of what hue, are with only a few exceptions more delicate and frail than the natural birds, and are generally also smaller and weaker; and furthermore, that their offspring is less numerous, and that imperfect development of some organs is not rare, it is clear that we have to deal with a symptom of degeneration.

The symptoms of degeneration seem to increase the more, as the colouring of the variety differs from the colouring of the natural bird. So we still find among the naturally-coloured "blue blood" Budgerigars strong birds, which sometimes even surpass the natural bird in size. The smallest and most weakly ones are the sky-blue Budgerigars—probably also the very rare white ones—the size of which is mostly a third smaller than the size of the normal bird.

Besides the symptoms of degeneration mentioned above, there is still another externally perceptible one, especially in the case of the blue variety, the imperfection of the wings which also appears in natural birds degenerated by in-breeding. The wings are, in many cases, incompletely feathered. These stunted birds, it is unnecessary to say, are unsuitable for breeding. Unfortunately they are bought and sold as "young sky-blue Budgerigars."

There are other symptoms of degeneration. "The females often suffer from laying difficulties, the eggs are often smaller than those of the green birds, the number of sterile eggs in a clutch is comparatively larger and rearing of the young is not always easy. Particularly strongly-built young ones in the nest which surpass their brothers and sisters in size to the satisfaction of the breeder, turn out eventually to be green throw-backs when the feathers are grown."

" Further, the bad habits of hens in destroying clutches and broods of others, scarcely observed in the case of imported birds and in isolated cases only among ordinary Budgerigars bred in Europe, seems to be the rule in the case of highly-bred coloured varieties " (Stefani in *Jahrbuch* 1925 der A.Z.).

The dangers of degeneration must be counteracted by the breeder in every direction. This is done by following the advice given about the choice of birds for breeding. Then he must provide for coloured Budgerigars as favourable conditions as possible. This consists in keeping each couple apart in very wide cages which allow as much freedom of movement as possible. Stefani affirms that a minimum length of 3 ft. 6 in. per cage for one couple is necessary and this cage must be placed on a balcony or verandah or in any case in the open during the warm season. Better still is a garden aviary or something like it, at least 6 ft. long. When the birds hibernate in the open, which can be done when the aviary is placed in a sheltered situation or can be protected by such measures as windows, etc., the area should be still larger.

Mr. Richard Schwarzkopf, of Ingelfingen, says in *Gef. Welt*, 1924: " To notice the first signs of degeneration in the broods requires a sharp eye and thorough knowledge in the breeder. It is possible to avoid difficulties by letting nature have its own way as much as possible. Man is not able to recognise the morphological qualities of the live animal and the physiological qualities only after long observation. Therefore free selection is to my mind the method which will lead in the quickest and most certain way to the end in view. For nature alone carries out the complementary measures necessary for preservation of the races in pairing the individuals. The yellow variety of the

Budgerigar is according to authorities without any doubt a product of in-breeding, if it is not already a symptom of degeneration. Therefore this variety is frail and delicate. It is different with the blues. At least I have hibernated so-called "blue-blood" Budgerigars—sky-blue beneath and partially blue up to the crop—in an open-air aviary, and in spite of cold and snow I brought up several broods. In the spring there is great activity, up to six young ones have flown out of one nest and the percentage of birds of blue extraction is high. In order to supply fresh blood I am willing to effect exchanges with owners of blue Budgerigars . . . but I certainly believe that it will be possible to produce blue Budgerigars in this way also in Germany." It will scarcely be possible, however, always to allow "free selection" as probably most of the breeders do not possess material for breeding in such abundance that they are able to apply free selection. Besides it appears doubtful whether this free selection would really produce the effects Mr. Schwarzkopf assumes.

But attention may be drawn to his reference to the supply of fresh blood and a union of all breeders of coloured Budgerigars with common interests in order to render the supply of fresh blood possible. Renewal of blood, that is crossing with unrelated individuals of another strain may have good results as regards size, vitality and fertility. In-breeding, that is the pairing of parents with their own offspring, or pairing of brothers and sisters, preserves the peculiarity of the coloured variety, but leads to more or less rapid degeneration which can be prevented by the supply of fresh blood.

In order to obtain the desired success a breeder of coloured Budgerigars must know the laws of heredity. Mr. Schwarzkopf (in another publication) says quite rightly that he who claims to be a breeder to-day ought to be familiar with the Mendelian laws of heredity, whether he breeds animals or cultivates plants. If he does not know them, his pairing is only playing instead of breeding and the products of his cross-breeding are only products of chance which may be very valuable in the hands of the experienced breeder, but are useless for breeding purposes in the hands of the layman. If one wishes to reach one's aim there is required in addition to insight, the gift of observation and knowledge, as well as plenty of room and appliances for breeding. To find out whether an animal is surely homozygote or heterozygote requires individual treatment and many periods of breeding. Two animals are necessary for breeding and it may take a long time to ascertain which one is homozygote or heterozygote, and it can be very expensive too, unless the breeder is so lucky as to pair two homogeneous animals by chance. The dangers of in-breeding are added to those difficulties. A new line of breeding, in our case the colour of Budgerigars, cannot be reached without sensible in-breeding. Here the physique and the organic functions of the parent animals play the decisive part.

It is Mendel's great merit to have recognised that the hereditary tendencies of the parents do not amalgamate into entirely new ones different from those of the parents, but are preserved side by side.

Mendel made experiments chiefly with plants. But

it has been shown that the rules found for plants apply equally to the heredity of animals.

In the diagram given on p. 113 illustrating Mendel's laws of heredity we can see that in the first generation the characteristic of one parent, the red colour, is dominant (d.) over the characteristic of the other parent, the colourless white and the latter, though present, is recessive (r.) Mostly the original form will be dominant over the results of breeding. So when crossing naturally-coloured Budgerigars with coloured varieties the native colour will be dominant over the derived colour of the domestic state, which means that all young birds will be coloured naturally.

The descendants of this first generation will also show the natural colour dominant and that in the proportion of three to one. Thus three of the young birds would be naturally coloured and one only would show the colour of the derived domestic form.

But neither are the three naturally-coloured birds homogeneous. Only one would transmit the pure natural colour. In the two others the colour of the variety is present, but is recessive, and if these two were crossed the descendants (third generation) would be graduated again in the following proportion : one naturally coloured bird, two mixed (with the natural colour dominant and the colour of the variety recessive) and one bird having the colour of the variety. There are thus three quite different forms present in the proportion 1 : 2 : 1, two of which, however, only appear in the proportion 3 : 1. The birds which in these two generations already have their colour unmixed are called homozygote.

The birds which have one colour of their parents

dominant and the other one recessive, that is present, but not appearing, are heterozygote.

Both are of value to the breeder. The homozygotes are purely coloured birds of pure heredity when inbred ; the heterozygotes are used for breeding homozygotes, that is birds which transmit the pure colour. This is achieved by interbreeding heterozygotes with the result 1 : 2 : 1 or by crossing homozygotes with heterozygotes. The result is shown in the diagram.

This kind of heredity which is characterised by the dominance of either one or the other characteristic mark of the parents is called alternative heredity.

About another kind of heredity which does not show dominant and recessive characteristics, Dr. Braune says in a paper, " Colour-breeding of Budgerigars," published in *Gef. Welt*, 1923 : " Further investigations have shown that dominant and recessive characteristics appear by no means always in cross-breeding. If one interbreeds, for instance, the red-blossoming with the white-blossoming Marvel of Peru (Mirabilis jalapa) the blossom of the first cross-generation is without exception pink. These pink flowers, however, have pink as well as white and red offspring and that in the same proportion as the peas : one red and one white, both with purely coloured offspring, and two with pink blossoms which in their turn split up in exactly the same way. In this case, therefore, the pure specimens can be at once distinguished by their exterior from the cross-specimens, as the latter represent a compromise. From the exterior of the pink variety one would think that it is a real mixture of both colours, but the reappearance of the original red or white blossoms, as the case may be, in the following genera-

The law of Mendel in crossing red-and white-blossoming Peas (alternative heredity).

▦ = red-blossoming pea - red/red

□ = white-blossoming pea - white/white

First Generation.

All individuals are red. Formula red (d.)/white (r.)

Red is purely and absolutely dominant (d.)

White is recessive (r.) i.e. latently present but does not appear.

Second Generation.

$^1/_4$ of the individuals are red ($^1/_4$ unmixed, $^2/_4$ mixed) $^1/_4$ white.

Interbreeding of red/white × red/white thus produces the following $^1/_4$ red/red, red unmixed; $^1/_4$ red/white, red mixed; $^1/_4$ white/red, red mixed; $^1/_4$ white/white, unmixed white.

Third Generation.

Cross-breeding of homozygotes with heterozygotes.

96

tions clearly shows that in the generative cells the tendencies remained unmixed."

This kind of heredity is called "intermediary heredity."

In the paper in question Dr. Braune says further : " Now about our coloured Budgerigars. The natural primary colour is green with the well-known marks and designs in other colours. Yellow is albinism from green, so-called ' Xanthism ' as in the case of our canary, and is, according to the way in which it appears, to be considered as a pronounced mutation.*

"Absolutely yellow Budgerigars (total albinism) when paired together will always produce yellow offspring. If one obtains from yellow parents also green young, one may be sure that at least one of the parents is not ' pure,' that is, it shows only partial albinism.

* Among varieties, no matter whether in regard to colour or other characteristics, we make according to their origin two main distinctions—Variations and Mutations. The former kind presents itself as small and insignificant deviations from the characteristics of the parents. By casual—or in the case of artificial breeding, deliberately caused—coincidence of such (at first very small) variations in the parents, they can reappear in the children in a more marked degree. At last, after a series of generations, they may lead to pronounced marks deviating from the original form. So a bluish tint of the plumage can, by the pairing of two such parents, develop at last into a distinctly blue tone in the plumage of the young, which then becomes more or less constantly hereditary.

Much more quickly than variations, mutations have the same result. By mutations we mean the sudden deviations from characteristics of the parents appearing in the young ones as it were by leaps, which are often observed. To these belongs albinism characterised by a sudden appearance of white in hairs or feathers and red eyes, which points to the lack of the normal pigment in these structures.

Variations as well as mutations behave in the same way in regard to heredity, only mutations lead to the goal more quickly. Both are usually recessive in case of meeting with a normal consort. Their entire disappearance in the first generation therefore does not at all mean a failure to the breeder. The next generation will enlighten him about the real situation.

From yellows paired with absolutely green birds one may expect naturally coloured green ones; these, however, paired together or with unmixed yellow ones, will show the characteristics of heterozygotes—that means, they will produce yellow as well as green offspring in proportion. As, with regard to these proportional figures, we have of course always to deal with chance possibilities, the exact proportion cannot be obtained by a small, but only by a long series of experiments.

"Whether the glossy satin-coloured Budgerigars (or satin-greens as they are usually termed) must be considered as variations or mutations is undecided.

"The blue Budgerigars are most likely to have arisen by variation, i.e. by gradually breeding for a more intense blue colouring.

"The olive-green ones seem, according to Freytag, to be a mixed colour of blue and green. The blue-greens seem to possess the same potentialities, only the blue perhaps in a very small degree, but in this case the two colours do not appear mixed. Further breeding will probably bring more and more exact knowledge. This applies also to the jade greens which are said to be a product of crossing blue, yellow and green. Amateurs can still do a good deal of laudable work for science in this regard.

"The reader may guess the unlimited possibilities we have to deal with in such breeding experiments. The breeding of coloured varieties of the Budgerigar is no simple matter, but all the greater is the interest of the breeder and the pleasure which success gives."

OLIVE-GREEN BUDGERIGARS are probably the result of systematical selection from yellow Budgerigars with an olive-green tinge. They are distinguished from the naturally coloured bird only by the pronounced olive-coloured tone of the green plumage. The olive-green is sometimes brighter, sometimes darker. Also in another way, however, have olive-green Budgerigars been produced of a very dark shade, as well as light or emerald-greens and beautiful dark greens with a bluish shade and blue under tail-coverts, and " sky-blues." The following communication from Mr. Mayer of Lucerne (*Gef. Welt*, 1924) gives the following information on this point : " In the years 1916 and 1917 many hundred couples of green Budgerigars passed through my hands intended for export to America. My critical eye soon discovered several birds among them showing a distinctly blue gloss. I thought here was a fine opportunity, carefully picked out those specimens and already imagined a flight of these beautiful blue Budgerigars. But alas! As these birds with undoubted blue blood were a bit small and weakly, and I feared crippled offspring, I made the great mistake of inter-breeding them with the big strong green Budgerigars from my own stock, and so I had to wait full five years till the blue blood was dominant again. At last in June, 1922, the memorable event happened. During an inspection of one of the nests in the room where I keep the birds for breeding I noticed two sky-blue Budgerigars and two dark olive-green ones. In the next brood were a sky-blue bird, an emerald-green one, and a dark green one. In the third brood were four birds, but all of them a nice dark-green with a bluish tinge. That was all! Once while feeding, the male of the couple was struck by apoplexy and died. Last year I replaced it by one of the dark green sons of the first brood after the mother had refused pairing with the blue son. The result was good. The first brood yielded two sky-blue birds and two dark green ones and the second brood five green ones, two of them light or emerald-green, three of them dark green. This year I have mated five couples, avoiding as much as possible too near relationship, all with strongly blue blood, while two of the females were an unmixed blue. Now I have already twenty-four young birds, strong healthy specimens, but none of them a pure sky-blue, but I still hope to get sky-blue ones. They are partly emerald-green, partly dark green, partly tending towards an olive-green hue, but all with a decided blue tinge and an almost clear blue plumage at the under-surface of the tail. It is interesting that in three places in Switzerland, where I had disposed of some of my green birds of last year and the year before, a blue one has been bred this year. It is by no means easy to breed distinctly blue ones from green Budgerigars and the inter-bred blue birds are weakly, soon degenerate and the colour fades, which means that they soon turn whitish till at last they become a clear white. Only by mixing with blue blood is that rich deep sky-blue colour obtained which is so beautiful."

The dangers of degeneration have been avoided by Mr. Mayer by " letting nature have its way as much as possible." But I do not believe that by breeding in this way alone the aim of breeders of coloured varieties will be realised.

The JADE-COLOURED BUDGERIGAR is a coloured variety of particular beauty. To produce it, naturally coloured yellow and blue Budgerigars are said to have been used. Mr. Stefani proposes in "*Jahrbuch* 1925 der A.Z." to call it the May-green Budgerigar: "In the foliage of birch trees in May one would entirely overlook the bird, as it is coloured exactly like the leaves." The dark pencilling is of a grey-green colour. Mr. Freytag, of Wiesbaden, obtained by cross-breeding " jade-coloured " and " blue blood Budgerigars," green young ones with light blue abdomen.

SATIN-GREEN BUDGERIGARS are described by Mr. Lichtenstaedt as " splendidly coloured birds. The abdomen is a deep shining green beautifully resplendent in the sun, one of the prettiest parrots . . ." Young birds of this variety distinguish themselves from the naturally coloured bird by a slightly darker green. A " slightly " bluish tinge of the plumage of the under parts I have never been able to observe. Sellers saw it. The gloss is said to develop only at a greater age. They are said to be bigger and stronger than the natural birds.

As a throw-back resulting from pairing olive-green Budgerigars, Mr. Stefani in another place mentions ORANGE-COLOURED BUDGERIGARS showing a rich yolk-yellow which suggests orange-colour. For the rest this variety resembles the yellow Budgerigar. It is a deeply coloured throw-back to this variety to which probably the olive-green ones owe their existence.

BLUE-BLOODED BUDGERIGARS are, as a rule, particularly large and strong birds resembling the natural bird, which they are said to surpass in size, with the exception of the plumage of the abdomen and sometimes also the under tail-coverts, which show a more or less distinct blue tinge. They represent reactions from breeding blue birds. Paired together, the blue-blood

Budgerigars produce naturally coloured young ones which probably, like their parents, are valuable for breeding the blue variety.

BLUE BUDGERIGARS. " No bird all over the world," reports Mr. van der Snickt in 1881, " has caused so much admiration and at the same time so many expectations as the blue Budgerigar of Mr. L. of Uccle. This bird is quite free from yellow with the exception of the bill, which appears yellowish ; the head is snow-white with pitch-dark design, eye-ball white, iris black ; back black, blue and ashy-grey ; breast sky-blue. This was a male bird, and was paired with a yellow female. The young ones obtained were all yellow. In the course of the summer (1881) Mr. K., also of Uccle, bred another blue Budgerigar, a female, which was blue all over its body. Head and tail, however, were yellow. Unfortunately the two blue birds were not paired ; the female is now brooding with a yellow male. I had also heard of two blue females and both were promised me. But when I arrived to fetch them, I found both lying dead on their eggs and already in such a state of decomposition that I could not stuff them.

" Now at last I have obtained the female I desired so long from the couple which, three years ago, brought forth the male. It is not yet quite perfectly coloured, but it is already plain that it will be as pretty as the older one."

The SKY-BLUE BUDGERIGARS, rather widely bred nowadays, show a nice sky-blue where the natural bird is green, and the yellow part of the plumage has turned into white. Otherwise it is just like the natural bird. The birds offered for sale as " COBALT-BLUES " show a dark blue plumage. There are also blue Budgerigars, which still show a clear yellow, particularly at the head.

The first blue Budgerigars excited the ecstasy of bird-lovers. Mr. Pracht describes in *Gef. Welt*, 1924, the impression the birds made on him : "The long cherished hope is fulfilled. Before me is an observation-cage with the precious contents—a couple of absolutely blue Budgerigars. Everybody who sees them is as enchanted as I am. All fears that the blue ones would only differ in colour from the natural bird, but that the colour would not equal the very pretty primitive bird, are extinguished. The blue Budgerigars combine the beauty of the green one with the green replaced by a marvellous sky-blue. When once the blue ones are as easy to breed as the other varieties and, therefore, become more accessible and cheaper, then the verdict may be changed, as experience teaches. Whatever appears in large quantities, though ever so pretty, soon suffers neglect. The colour of the blue Budgerigar is distributed as follows : where the primitive bird is green the blue artificially-bred bird is blue. On the tail-coverts the blue colour also has the metallic gloss of the green bird. Where the primitive bird is yellow (upper head, throat and edges of the wing-feathers, feathers of the wing-coverts, edges of the eyelids) the blue Budgerigar is a creamy white. The throat shows the clearest white. The little beard is a deep dark-blue, the dots on the throat a still deeper blue. The bill is like the primitive bird's. Differences due to sex are also the same. The feet are delicately pink and almost transparent. The claws are grey. The eyes black. Where the primitive bird has the black rippled marking the blue, the artificially-bred bird has a very delicate grey, almost dun marking. The long tail-feathers are analogous to the green bird's, but all blue. In their singing, chirping, chattering with each other, feeding each other—in short, in their general behaviour, they closely resemble the primitive bird. How could it be otherwise? They have the same body and the same instincts as the primitive birds. Breeding only gave them another pigment or withheld a part of the pigment, or mixed them otherwise, as the result of the intervention of the breeder. The product of this intervention is so charming that, as mentioned before, I am not the only enthusiastic follower. One of the Budgerigars is just shaking up its plumage and between the wing-coverts the upper back, rump and the upper feathers of the tail-coverts become visible and show their glittering blue splendours. These parts bear comparison with the shining parts of the plumage of the king-fisher."

The experience hitherto of German breeders with the blue-coloured variety shows that without systematic breeding the producing of blue Budgerigars is merely a matter of chance. The results of breeding published below show that clearly.

Dr. Mayer, of Lucerne, obtained blue birds by cross-breeding blue-blood birds and natural birds. The result was:

First brood: Two sky-blue birds, two olive-green ones.

Second brood: One sky-blue bird, one emerald (light) green one, one dark-green one.

Third brood : Four dark-greens with a bluish tinge. One of the dark-green young ones mated with the naturally coloured mother :

First brood : Two sky-blue birds, two dark-green ones.

Second brood : Two light-green birds, three dark-green ones.

An attempt with five birds bearing a strong strain of blue-blood, among them two sky-blue females, yielded :

Twenty-four young birds of different varieties of green, no sky-blue bird.

Mr. Lichtenstaedt, of Berlin, obtained from a highly blue-blood couple with intensely light-blue under-surface :

Four young ones with a delicate green on the upper-surface which seemed as it were powdered with blue. The under-surface was intensely sky-blue. They developed into naturally coloured birds, only a little blue on the under-surface remaining.

Mr. Schwarzkopf, of Ingelfingen, bred from Budgerigars with blue blood " a good percentage of birds with blue heredity."

According to the other statements sky-blue Budgerigars are said to be produced by inter-breeding birds of blue blood with olive-coloured ones.

All this shows that these products of chance do not make us achieve the desired object.

WHITE BUDGERIGARS.—Dr. E. Rey, many years ago, observed among the birds bred by him a variety with a broad, clear, white stripe across the wings. At the same time the plumage was on the whole of a duller hue, the green was more bluish and the blue more slate-coloured.

In 1897 L. van der Snickt, of Brussels, related that breeding of yellow Budgerigars also yielded birds with partially white feathers.

" These latter do not form a constant variety, they are the same as the yellow ones with a slightly green gloss on the back and breast, the whole plumage canary-yellow, no traces of pencilling nor the dots at the throat ; the spots on the cheeks are white, and gleam like silver; the tips of the tail and the wings are white, bill and feet are flesh-coloured, eyes red, nostrils reddish. It seems peculiar that among seven birds with red eyes and white spots on the cheeks which I had occasion to observe I did not find a single male. Would that be accidental ? All the young ones of these albinos paired with green males were green ; one exception only resembled the female."

The white variety is rarely to be found. The plumage is a clear white with a fine gloss. The design which is black in the case of the natural bird is here a dim lustre-less white.

Mr. Stefani mentioned in another place also MOUSE-COLOURED BUDGERIGARS, probably impurely coloured birds of the white variety.

MAUVE BUDGERIGARS mentioned by Mr. Mayer, of Lucerne, in *Gef. Welt*, 1924, have come from sky-blue birds. Their ground-colour is a bright violet-blue with a touch of pink.

DARK CREAM-COLOURED BUDGERIGARS were bred by Mr. Lichtenstaedt, of Berlin, by systematical selection from yellow birds. In perfectly coloured condition they had about the colour of young newly-fledged yellow Budgerigars.

BLACK-HEADED BUDGERIGARS have been offered for sale by a Liverpool firm. I do not know whether we have here to deal with a product of chance or a result of colour-feeding. Probably the latter. Mr. Stefani reports (in another place) that a bird lover in the Rhine provinces possessed " two green colour-fed Budgerigars, one of which has a beautifully fiery red, the other a brownish-red head, otherwise their natural plumage is quite unchanged." The endeavour to obtain coloured varieties of the Budgerigar by colour-feeding is a useless pastime for breeders of Budgerigars, as pigments would have to be administered continually in order to preserve the colours thus obtained. Unfavourable results would be sure to follow.

YELLOW BUDGERIGARS.—The first traces of flavism were discovered in the bird which was bred by Dr. Rey and described above, a Budgerigar with a white stripe across the wings. This cross-stripe gradually turned yellow. An almost canary-yellow Budgerigar was bred by Mr. Stechmann, director of the zoological garden of Breslau, with the following markings : the young bird showed upper-surface dim and pale, greyish-green-yellow, edge of forehead intensely yellow, with indistinct dark cross stripes ; upper head, sides of the head and neck, pale grey-green cross stripes ; nape and upper back pale-grey with bright yellow spots. Central and lower back and rump a clear glittering grass-green; primaries feebly yellowish-white, exterior vane more intensely yellowish, tip dark-grey, secondaries more vividly yellow with broad grey tips, the first wing-feathers on the under-surface almost

clear white, the rest yellow-white, all with grey tips ;
feathers of the first wing-coverts bright yellow with
grey tips ; all other feathers of upper wing-coverts
irregularly grey with yellow spots, the small under wing-
coverts yellow-green, the large ones yellow, on the right
wing grey ; upper tail-coverts greenish-yellow ; tail
feathers yellow, the two central ones pale yellow, the
others more vivid, all with bluish-green tips and dark
ribs, on the under-surface likewise bright yellow, all with
grey tips ; beard vividly yellow, the blue spots small and
delicate, vague on the left side only, the blackish spots
small and delicate ; neck and throat bright yellow ;
breast and belly yellowish-green ; sides and thighs a
clearer green ; central part of the belly, hind-quarters
and under tail-coverts blue-green; bill horny grey-white;
feet grey-white. Size at least a third smaller than
the natural bird. In the birdroom of Mr. Stechmann
there was also an extremely pretty and strong male,
the two central tail-feathers of which appeared bright
yellow instead of blue.

" I do not doubt," thus Mr. L. van der Snickt wrote
me in 1878, " that the Budgerigar, like the canary, will
produce different races and varieties in a comparatively
short time. For more than ten years past Mr. Kessels
in Uccle (Holland), one of our most important lovers
and breeders, has possessed extremely large and strong
Budgerigars, bred by him in such a way that every
time he saw a female which was a little larger than
usual he bought it and put it into his breeding-cage.
Last winter about ten of his Budgerigars were stolen,
and when, somewhat later, strikingly large Budgerigars
came on the market, he immediately recognised his own
and was able to give up the thieves to the police. The

first yellow Budgerigars I saw as early as 1872 were in possession of Mr. T. Boone, among 150 naturally coloured couples. I wished to buy them, but they were not for sale. Then I advised keeping the yellow ones apart, together with the adult which reared them ; however, they all perished accidentally. The second case was a yellow couple in a flight of more than 200 couples in Brussels ; this was sold to a lady for 500 francs, after which yellow young ones came out of the same nesting box again. In the summer of 1877 I counted in a small aviary, among fifty couples, fourteen yellow birds ; not all were, however, a clear yellow, some of them were greenish at the belly and back. Through the intervention of a dealer we brought fifty young ones out of the same cage the next autumn in order to continue breeding in a special room. Unfortunately, they all died shortly afterwards. In the zoological garden of Antwerp, there is also a similar variety but not a clear yellow." Later on (in 1878) the same author writes : " In this year more success has been obtained with yellow Budgerigars. One can divide them into the real yellow variety and albinos (mentioned above). Recently, however, I discovered in an aviary an entirely yellow female with here and there a dark green feather at the breast and almost black stripes on the wings. At a public sale in Antwerp there were also six yellow Budgerigars. These young birds were a dirty greenish-yellow with pale grey undulations and did not look pretty. Four of them have been bought by Mr. Westerman, director of the Zoological Garden of Amsterdam. The rest are in my possession. Another variety seems to be quite yellow at first sight, but when looking closely one notices a slight greenish gloss and on the neck and back traces of greenish-grey undulations ; beard-spots slightly blue, tips of the wings and of the tail white. Another variety is brimstone-coloured all over the body with very pale grey undulations on the neck and back ; the black spots of the throat are grey, spot on the cheek pale blue, feet flesh coloured, eyes black ; the male has a blue cere. From one couple Mr. Kessels bred in two broods at first one, then three young birds. Mme. Bodinus, who obtained a couple from me, has also bred twice, each time five young ones. All these young birds resemble their parents, only they are more regularly yellow.

" Only twice I saw yellow Budgerigars with black marks. One is stuffed, the second is the property of Mr. K. This gentleman has specialised in breeding canary-coloured Budgerigars without any undulations and with red eyes. In the spring he wanted to bet that he would obtain twenty-five a year. He succeeded, but, as I warned him beforehand, all twenty-five turned out to be females. Although 150 francs apiece have been offered him he will part with none of them. He hopes that it will be possible eventually to breed pure yellow males without undulations and with red eyes."

Mr. Hauth, of Potsdam, in 1881, obtained from a couple of yellow Budgerigars at first a dark yellow male. The ripple, however, was still visible. A second brood yielded seven young out of ten eggs, five of which became fledged ; three males were again a vivid yellow, one male and one female pale yellow. Mr. H. paired three males with newly imported green females, and the pale yellow female with an almost blue-yellow male. Unfortunately we did not receive any further report about the result of these efforts.

Meanwhile the yellow Budgerigar has become a constant type, a race, and reversions to the natural type are rare in rational breeding.

A successful breeder of yellow Budgerigars published detailed reports about these birds in *Gef. Welt*, 1904 : " There still remain two principal colour varieties, the bright yellow or brimstone-coloured ones with white wing-feathers and tail-feathers and white-bluish spots at the throat and cheeks, and the dark-yellow birds which also have white tail- and wing-feathers, but darker and more distinct blue spots at the throat and cheeks, and which are a much greater rarity. Feet and bill are identical in the two types, the former being flesh-coloured, the latter, as also the colour of the cere, the same as with the natural bird. The under-surface of the bright yellow ones has mostly a vague greenish hue which appears more intense on the lower part of the back and rump. No green tinge is to be noticed on the dark yellow (sometimes almost yolk-coloured) birds. The latter is the prettier form. Moreover, these birds are always bigger and stronger than the bright yellow ones. When the two types are paired together, they bring forth beautiful offspring. The very young newly-fledged birds show as long as they are still black-eyed the most beautiful yellow colour without any marks, which, however, with advancing years appear more distinctly. I am referring to the dark undulations on the upper surface which is never quite absent in old birds. These markings are, as it were, powdered with yellow and suffused with a feeble green gloss. At the age of about two or three months the young get light pearl-grey eyes (just like the green ones) and at the same time the undulations on the upper surface become noticeable, which were somewhat indistinct at first, just as the blue cere of the male and the greenish-brown one of the female, which in both sexes was almost reddish at first, later on turns a pale blue. An experienced breeder of Budgerigars can infallibly distinguish the sexes at the age of two months only.

"There is also a third colour variety of these Budgerigars, that is an impure greyish-yellow, with the undulations at the upper-surface distinctly present, but of a faded greyish-black. The fore head of these birds is a pale yellow, wing- and tail-feathers are dark. Undersurface and rump are almost greenish with a feeble yellow gloss. The blue spots on the throat and cheeks are present, but pale blue. Thus on the whole they are like the natural bird only much paler and growing yellowish. At first these birds were bred by chance from the green ones, later on they were also obtained as offspring from the yellow ones. They are a reversion to the primitive type. I frequently tried breeding with such birds in order to see the results. Mostly they produced greyish-yellow but never quite green young ones."

Breeding has to be carried out in the same way as with green ones. They also nest in every season. But the yellow Budgerigar is weaker than the green one and must hibernate in a warm room with a temperature of about 60 degrees. Even more than with green birds it is necessary to supply fresh blood when breeding the yellow type: " A very important factor in breeding yellow Budgerigars is the supply of fresh blood, therefore the breeder has to buy periodically, good new birds for breeding ; but he must not sell his own breeding couples and continue breeding with the newly acquired couples ; that would be useless, he should rather take the male of one couple, the female of another one and replace these by birds of another strain. The birds to be rejected should generally be the oldest or those which did not prove useful for breeding or are of a less pure colour. Further it has to be considered that the new birds should be perfect in all respects. They must be equivalent to one's own breeding-race in all respects, and if possible still better. The purchase of such birds has therefore to be made very cautiously. The best way is to get the birds for that purpose from a reliable breeder of yellow Budgerigars whose name is well known among fanciers or breeders. One should exchange birds with such breeders, as the breeder knows his birds better than the dealer. If, however, one has no other resource than dealers, it is wise not to buy all from the same, but rather from different traders, e.g. the males from one and the females from another. Thus one makes pretty sure that the acquired birds are not brothers and sisters or too nearly related, which otherwise may happen quite easily, as dealers often buy their birds all from the same source. I always went about it in this way when breeding yellow Budgerigars and it always proved right. I was able to avoid the pernicious degeneration I so frequently saw at so many breeders. The breeding of yellow Budgerigars was very profitable in former years when high prices were still paid for these birds."

Ailments and Their Treatment

Signs of Illness : Loss of vivacity.—Languid, lustreless eyes.—Ruffled plumage, hopping about indolently or sitting motionless with the head bent down.—Suddenly developing tameness.—Wet, dirty or sticky nostrils.—Panting, when not the result of excitement or anxiety.—Producing smacking noises audible in the stillness of the evening.—Puffiness of the breast and belly.—Emaciation.—Deeply sunk, wrinkled and discoloured, or sodden, blistery or inflamed abdomen.—Anal plumage soiled with droppings.—Unnatural condition of droppings. In the ordinary course these consist of two parts, a thick blackish-green and a smaller white. In case of sickness droppings are thin, watery, slimy, greasy, discoloured, evil-smelling.

Treatment of Suspected Illness.—Any bird suspected of disease should be isolated in a cage in a quiet spot. The usual mode of feeding should be continued till one succeeds in diagnosing the disease, though all kinds of stimulating food should be withheld. The Budgerigar suspected of illness only receives white millet. No bathing-water is given to sick Budgerigars.

Diagnosis is often difficult. One must observe the bird and compare its condition with the symptoms described below. If medicines must be used, one should always use the simplest at first. If after conscientious examination one comes to the conclusion that recovery is impossible, one should release the bird from its sufferings by killing it quickly.

Contagious Diseases.—One bird suffering from a contagious disease endangers the whole stock. In case of such disease all the birds must be caught and examined carefully, the sick and suspected being accommodated in special cages. The infected cage or birdroom with all its belongings is cleaned and disinfected. The most efficient disinfectants are boiling water, permanganate of potash, lysol and creolin. If strongly smelling disinfectants are used the cage should be rinsed well, birdroom and aviary must be whitewashed anew, the soil of the aviary must be dug up and renewed. During feeding the utmost precaution is necessary, lest the owner transmits the disease. The apparently healthy birds must always be taken care of at first.

Administering Medicine.—This is a difficult operation. Force should be avoided. Most medicines are administered to the Budgerigar in its drinking-water. As soon as it feels thirsty it will take the offered medicine. Warm drink is given once or twice a day. Before cooling down it should be removed.

Disease of the Respiratory Organs.—Keeping the birds in warm damp air is in many cases a remedy for this. Warm damp air is provided by surrounding the cage with leafy plants and by sprinkling these several times a day with lukewarm water by means of a spray while the room has a temperature of 68 to 86 degrees.

Colds (catarrh of the mucous membrane of the nose and throat).—*Causes :* Draught, icy cold drinking water, sudden change of temperature. Symptoms : Sneezing, yellow slimy discharge from the nostrils gathering in crusts, drooping of the head, bringing up of slime, tears in the eyes. *Remedies :* Daubing with grease, daubing the bill and throat with a solution of chlorate of potassium (1 : 100) ; cleaning the bill and the nostrils with a feather dipped in salted water, daubing with oil, steaming.

Catarrh of the Wind-pipe (Inflammation of the throat, laryngitis).—*Causes:* As above. *Symptoms:* Hoarseness, coughing, accelerated breathing, rattling in the throat, gaping. *Remedies:* In light cases slightly warmed drinking-water, honey and sugar-candy ; daubing the bill well down to the throat, and the nostrils with a solution of salicylic acid in water (1 : 500). Keep in warm damp atmosphere.

Pneumonia.—*Symptoms:* Breathing difficult or short, accompanied by a wheezing sound with wide opened bill, hot breast, dejection, loss of appetite, fever, coughs, expectoration of yellow slime sometimes streaked with blood, smacking noises. *Remedies:* Damp warm atmosphere as above, purified saltpetre (0.02-0.03 gr. in water) to be administered every three hours ; also some nitrate of sodium in the drinking-water and the remedies given for catarrh of the wind-pipe.

Pneumonia caused by fungoid growths mostly attended with inflammation of the intestines is incurable and contagious.

Tuberculosis is mostly the result of hereditary tendencies and appears in the lungs, the liver, the heart, the pericardium, the spleen, the kidneys, the stomach, the ovaries, the intestines, etc., and is always incurable. *Symptoms:* Rapidly losing flesh, sometimes the formation of abscesses in different parts of the body; also the symptoms of pneumonia.

Diphtheria and Roup.—*Cause:* Vegetable parasites, etc. *Symptoms:* Coughing, sneezing, breathing heavily with open bill, shaking of the head, expectoration of unpleasant-smelling slime, swallowing difficulties, gasping for breath and increasing shortness of breath, snoring and rattling noises, increasing exhaustion, squatting on the floor with drooping wings and closed eyes (nearly always attended with intestinal catarrh, with watery slimy droppings), tremors and thirst. A yellow slimy greasy liquid comes out of the nostrils, consolidating into dark yellow or brownish crusts ; the eye-lids swell and stick together. Duration of the disease 2-3 weeks, but sometimes 60-70 days. Sick birds must be kept apart, as the disease is highly contagious. The curable form is not recognisable by keepers. When the above symptoms show themselves, recovery is impossible.

Diseases of the Stomach and other Digestive Organs.— A weak digestion, frequently in connection with emaciation. *Symptoms :* Loss of appetite, ill-coloured brown, solid or pulpy evil-smelling droppings, laziness, weakness. *Causes :* Unsuitable, bad or too abundant food with the consequent ill effects upon the gall and other digestive liquids. *Remedies :* Light food, little green fodder, a little salt and slightly warmed drinking-water. Strongly recommended is luke-warm red wine, about 3-5 drops in a little drinking-water.—Flatulency (emphysema) has the same causes and occurs mainly in case of young birds. In a light form it is curable by careful piercing of the flat white blistery swelling : the air escapes at slight pressure and then the spot is daubed with warmed oil. Young in the nest are wrapped in soft, loose cotton-wool. The parents of the sick young ones must be given little food. If appearing frequently, put pure hydrochloric acid in the drinking-water (1 : 100).

Diarrhœa.—Generally it is only a symptom of illness. *Signs :* Whitish or yellowish slimy droppings, sticking together of the plumage of the hindquarter, swollen, sometimes inflamed anus. *Remedies :* Instead of drinking-water, thin lukewarm gruel ; no vegetables ; heat ; daubing the abdomen and the inflamed anus with warm oil ; for every bird, daily one drop of tincture of opium in the drinking-water.—In case of dysentery, recognisable by violent pressing of the hind-quarter and rough, slimy, occasionally bloody droppings, one should adminster 2-3 drops castor oil with thin luke-warm gruel, also diluted tincture of rhubarb (3-5 drops in a little drinking-vessel daily) and oil-enemas (see constipation). The sticky hind feathers must be soaked and washed with warm water.

Abdominal Inflammation (inflammation of the stomach and intestines).—*Causes :* Bad or too abundant food, too fresh seeds, wet vegetables, too cold drinking-water, cold draughts. *Symptoms :* The abdomen sags and the bird wags its tail when easing itself ; swollen and red abdomen, protruding sternum ; droppings blackish-green, sour or evil-smelling ; loss of appetite, considerable thirst, sitting exhausted with ruffled feathers and drooping wings. In general the bird is continually near the food-box, rummaging among the seeds but not eating. *Remedies :* Accommodation in an evenly heated room (64-68 degrees) ; no soft food, soaked seeds, vegetables, fruit, etc., daily a drop of opium-solution or red wine in a little lukewarm drinking-water ; rice-water, burnt magnesia (must be mixed with water and offered as a thin gruel) : 1-2 drops of a solution of nitrate of silver (1 : 800) daily. In most cases the bird is lost. Danger of infection is possible.

Typhoid Fever (contagious)—*Cause :* Bacteria, micrococci. *Symptoms :* Violent diarrhœa, with droppings of white-yellow slime, which then become greenish and soil the abdomen, loss of appetite, sitting down exhausted with drooping wings, trembling, sometimes vomiting of a thin greenish fluid, violent thirst, shivering, highly ruffled feathers, death in convulsions. *Preventive measure :* 2 drops of a solution of ferrous sulphate (1 : 500) in the drinking-water. Scarcely curable.

Pyæmia (blood-poisoning by overloading the blood with carbonic acid).—Incurable, rare in case of Budgerigars.

White Diarrhœa.—*Symptoms :* The bird is languid,

depressed, refuses to take its food, weak digestion, droppings slimy, white. *Cause:* Want of food-stuffs containing lime. *Cure:* Supply of food containing lime.

Constipation has different causes. *Symptoms:* Frequent attempts to ease themselves, moving to and fro of the hind-quarters, ruffling of the feathers, dejection, want of appetite. *Remedies:* Mechanical intervention by means of an enema, that is, carefully pushing a pin's head dipped in warmed oil (castor oil and olive oil in equal portions) into the anus, also a water-enema by means of a rubber syringe with thin glass-tube, rounded at the point (difficult to carry out), administering of castor oil with gruel, 1-2 drops once or twice daily.

Emaciation (Phthisis).—Mostly a consequence of illness of the digestive or respiratory organs or any other parts. Cure by ascertaining and removing the different causes.

Obesity.—*Cause:* Neglect and careless feeding. *Signs:* Difficult breathing, coughing, moving heavily, hard or thick droppings, a very full and fat body, languid, wrinkled, inactive skin, bald spots. *Remedies:* Less food, many vegetables ; wide cage ; frequent bathing.

Gout, Gouty Arthritis.—*Causes:* Accumulation of uric acid in the joints. *Symptoms:* Diminishing of appetite, fever, swellings at the joints of the wings and feet ; at first these swellings are hard, red, very warm and painful, then they get soft and contain a liquid mixed with blood and matter ; later on the swellings become hard again and the contents are gelatinous and cheesy ; sometimes after weeks the joint recovers spontaneously, but usually it remains thicker ; in the other case gradual emaciation, anæmia (pale mucous membranes), violent diarrhœa occur and the bird dies from exhaustion. *Preventive measures:* Proper nourishment. *Remedies:* Warmth. When the swelling is inflamed and hot it can be cooled with a solution of vinegar in water or acetate of lead in water, the swelling is wrapped in tow and this is kept wet with the above-mentioned chemicals ; later on the joints are wrapped in warmed wool. If the swelling suppurates an incision has to be made, but on no account too early ; the swelling is then pressed out and daubed with a solution of carbolic acid (1 : 200) ; internally in both cases a dose of a solution of salicylic acid (1 : 500) in water.

Dropsy is very rare. *Symptoms :* At first breathing is rendered difficult, then the body swells and, in extreme cases, distinctly perceptible liquid in the swollen part. Incurable.

Diseases of the Heart, Liver, Spleen and Kidneys are hardly possible to recognise.

Spasms, Epileptic Fits.—*Symptoms :* ¡ The bird suddenly collapses amidst convulsions and flapping of the wings, begins to tremble, staggers, turns its eyes and twists its head, falls and kicks about vehemently. *Causes :* Excitement, fright, anxiety, also obesity ; a cage that is too small, too much heat of the stove or of the sun, unsatisfied sexual instinct, etc. *Remedies :* Change of food, more vegetables and fruit, cool, pure air, change of cage, cold water on the head, purgatives. During the fit one should take the bird in the hand and hold it upright so that it cannot hurt itself. If the fit only happens once, it does not mean much in most cases. But if recurring, remedies must be applied and the causes investigated and removed.

Laying Troubles. Egg-binding.—*Causes :* The female is too young, weakly, tired and ailing, too fat or worn out by too much consecutive brooding ; too high temperature, scarcity of food-stuffs containing lime necessary for the formation of the eggshell ; also disturbance during laying. *Preventive measures :* Avoidance of the causes, proper choice and treatment of females for breeding. *Remedies :* Warmth : the bird is wrapped in cloths, put into the cage near the stove, but not in an overheated place ; steam-baths. It has proved successful to direct a thin jet of cold water on to the abdomen of the bird for several minutes. Introduction of oil into the opening ; destruction of the egg is difficult to carry out and dangerous for the sick Budgerigar.

Apparatus for the application of steam-baths : Different sorts of apparatus for applying steam-baths are for sale. In the illustration below we show an apparatus that every fancier can easily make for himself and which serves its purpose quite well. It is made in the following way : A case made of smoothly planed well-fitting boards with a sliding top, has in the centre of one of the narrow sides a round opening (o). In the interior a ledge (b) is fixed against

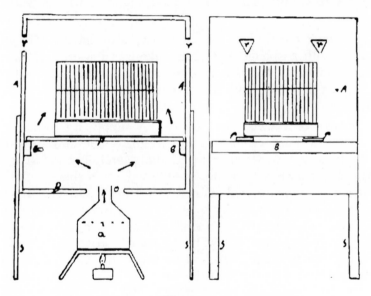

Fig. 31.

the two narrow sides, whereon rest two movable battens (p). The cage with the patient is put on these. The incisions (r) in these two sides serve as outlets for the steam. The four exterior corners of the case rest on four wooden legs (s), which must be high enough for a spirit-kettle (a) to stand underneath, the funnel-shaped top of which enters the case through the round opening (o). The whole is painted with oil-colour. It is advisable to replace the wooden top by a pane of glass.

Parasitic Worms.—The presence of these can hardly be recognised by the layman, therefore remedies are not to be advised. The birds apparently do not suffer much from them.

Rheumatic Complaints and painful paralysis occur in consequence of cold, in particular of draughts. *Remedies :* Rubbing the painful limb with warm oil and wrapping it in a warmed woollen cloth, and keeping the bird in a warm room.

Wounds mostly heal very quickly ; after having washed them with a sponge and clean luke-warm water, one has to clean them with tincture of arnica diluted with water (1 : 25-50) and daub them with oil and carbolic acid (1 : 200).

Fractures likewise heal easily. A simply fractured leg above the joint needs rest for healing. The two ends of the bone can be set right by handling carefully and putting the leg between two pieces of wood, or strips of cardboard ; these are tied with a soft thread and plaster or moderately warm sticky glue is spread over it ; the bird should not move till it has dried up and then be put in a narrow cage with a low, broad perch. After about four weeks the bandage is soaked in water and taken off. In case of simple fractures of the wing one applies cotton-wool over and under the wing after setting it in the natural position and then ties the wing, or better still both wings, tight to the body by means of narrow bandages. Serious fractures with external wounds are treated in the same way as wounds.

Abscesses.—Hard abscesses must be softened by a warm poultice ; a much inflamed (hot and red) swelling must be cooled with a solution of acetate of lead and then softened in the same way by a warm poultice which must often be renewed. A ripe abscess has to be opened up and pressed out, then daubed with carbolic acid (1 : 200) and bandaged if possible. **Atheromas** appear particularly on the head, near the bill, in the region of the eyes ; they are neither hard nor soft, filled with a skinny mass, and grow excessively or go deeper. As long as they are small or lie loose in the skin they can easily be removed by cauterising with nitrate of silver or by ligature, using a strong thin thread. Mostly atheromas result from the corruption of interior liquids. In such cases the bird can only be saved by withdrawal of all unnatural food ; a dose of a solution of salicylic acid (1 : 100 hot water) to be taken for 3 or 6 weeks may be effective.

Swellings of the Conjunctiva, Conjunctivitis, are produced by cold and are an attendant condition of other complaints. *Symptoms :* Tears in the eyes, swelling of the eye-lids, dread of light. *Remedies :* Daubing with luke-warm chloric liquid (1 : 500) or a solution of alum (1 : 500) or sulphate of zinc (1 : 600).—Conjunctivitis or inflammation of the cornea may set in when the eye is hit or bitten. *Remedies :* Cooling with water, daubing with a solution of sulphate of zinc, with opium (1 : 200).

Deformation of the Bill.—If the upper part of the bill projects so far over the under part, that it becomes a hindrance while taking food, it should, after repeated rubbing with warm oil, be cut to its normal length by means of a sharp knife. A split in the horn of the bill is cleaned once a day by means of a brush with warm soap-water and smeared with warm oil.—An apparently normal bill sometimes, after being hurt, begins to grow excessively at the tip, frequently splitting up into fibres. *Cause :*

Faulty nutrition of the horn. It has to be cut to the right size by means of scissors. Natural nourishment, addition of lime, sand, avoiding of soft food are the only remedies.

Foot-diseases.—On the neglected foot of a bird there easily appear under a crust of dirt inflammation, suppuration or ulcers which may lead to inflammation of the joints, mortifying of toes, even loss of the foot. If the inflamed foot is bathed in warm water early, cooled with solution of acetate of lead, the inflamed spots smeared daily with diluted glycerine (1 : 10) and then powdered thickly with the finest starch-flour, a quick recovery is probable.— It is more difficult to remove callosities from which arise sores in the joints or corns. Treatment as mentioned above. *Cause:* Too thin, hard or otherwise defective perches. The corn must be softened by applying warm olive-oil and washing with warm soap-water, then cut out cautiously with a little knife. Further treatment is like that of wounds, and may be supplemented by cauterising with nitrate of silver.—If round the joint of a foot a tough sharp fibre has developed, which by incision has caused inflammation and suppuration, it has to be treated as above and the fibre removed by means of pointed scissors ; the foot heals spontaneously after glycerine-ointment has been spread on it. Foot-sore Budgerigars are given blotting-paper instead of sand as floor-covering of the cage, and comfortable perches.

Overlong toe nails should be cut shorter. It is important not to cut into the quick of the toe. The toe is held against the light in order to see how far the flesh reaches, and is cut considerably below that point.

Crumbling or Splitting of the Toe Nails is caused by over-coddling or illness. The brittle parts may be cut off carefully.

Diseases of the Plumage.—*Causes:* Lack of cleanliness, warm dry air of the room, lack of bathing accommodation, obesity, disease of the gland at the root of the tail, scarcity of feather-forming materials in the food, microscopic parasites of animal or vegetable nature settling in the skin or in the feathers. When the causes are known, the way to recovery is easy. For extermination of the parasites see Chap. viii. Bald spots suddenly appearing are sometimes quickly covered with feathers again if smeared thinly every other day with carbolic acid (1 : 100) or glycerine.

Plucking of their own plumage, gnawing at their own wings and toes is rare among Budgerigars. The causes are neglect, in consequence of which corruption of the blood sets in. Cure very difficult, most likely to be effected gradually by proper care.

Lightning Source UK Ltd.
Milton Keynes UK
UKOW04f2232080714

234819UK00001B/105/P